Full of Hope

Full of Hope

Critical Social Perspectives on Theology

EDITED BY
MAGDALA THOMPSON

Paulist Press
New York/Mahwah, N.J.

Cover design by Valerie Petro
Book design by Lynn Else

Library of Congress Cataloging-in-Publication Data

Full of hope : critical social perspectives on theology / edited by Magdala Thompson.
    p. cm.
    Includes bibliographical references.
    ISBN 0-8091-4121-3 (alk. paper)
    1. Feminist theology—Congresses. 2. Feminism—Religious aspects—Catholic Church—Congresses. 3. Sociology, Christian (Catholic)—Congresses. I. Thompson, Magdala.
BX1795.F44 F85 2003
230'.082—dc21

                                      2003001689

Published by Paulist Press
997 Macarthur Boulevard
Mahwah, New Jersey 07430

www.paulistpress.com

Printed and bound in the United States of America

Contents

Preface vii
Magdala Thompson

1. Feminist Theology: The Heart of the Matter.................1
   Mary Aquin O'Neill

2. Feminism and Hope 20
   Margaret A. Farley

3. Freedom, Emancipation, and Deliverance:
   Toward a Theology of Freedom 41
   M. Shawn Copeland

4. Feminism and the Sacredness of Place................74
   Rosemary Luling Haughton

5. Feminist Theology, Catholicism, and the Family 94
   Lisa Sowle Cahill

6. Fixing Public Schools:
   A Catholic Feminist Analysis.........................112
   Christine E. Gudorf

List of Contributors 149

I know the plans I have in mind for you—it is Yahweh who speaks—plans full of peace, not disaster, reserving a future full of hope for you.

Jeremiah 29:11

Preface

This is a book about hope, in which six well-known feminist theologians express their hope for a future of equality for women and men in many fields—religion, education, family, society, ecology, and the realm of the heart.

During my nearly twenty years as a marriage and family therapist, I have become increasingly aware of the fact that many abused wives have been held captive by a religious culture that prized the masculine control of the family above the dignity of equal partnership. In the face of emotional and even physical abuse from their spouses, many of these women were urged by representatives of their respective churches to keep in mind that "love conquers all."

In southern Alabama there have been few women theologians to provide and model a sound theological base for full equality. For this reason, Sister Dominica Hyde, R.S.M., and I sought and were given a grant from the Sisters of Mercy of the Baltimore Region to bring, from 1995 to 2000, feminist theologians to Mobile for a series of lectures on feminist theology. We wanted to assure women that there is no theological basis for inequality.

We found enthusiastic agreement from Rev. Christopher Viscardi, S.J., Chairman of the Theology Department at Spring Hill College, and from Sister Sandra

Ardoyno, S.L., President of the Sisters' Council of Mobile, for joint sponsorship of the series by Spring Hill College, the Sisters of Mercy, and the Sisters' Council of Mobile.

Under the aegis of Christus/Mercy, six fall lectures were presented at Spring Hill College in Mobile by some of the best feminist theologians in the country. Responses on the part of large audiences have led us to believe that the seeds planted will bear fruit. While the authors call on scripture, church history, papal letters, and modern research, each essay is related to the writer's respective area of expertise and experience. All offer solid grounds for both attitudinal and policy changes toward a fuller realization of equality.

I want to thank the Sisters of Mercy, and the members of the program committee who selected the speakers and for the most part the specific topics: Sister Sandra Ardoyno, S.L., Sister Susan Hébert, R.S.M., Sister Dominica Hyde, R.S.M., Ms. Deborah Madonia, Ms. Cathy O'Keefe, and Dr. Kathleen Orange.

I am indebted to Thomas E. Clarke, S.J., and to Margaret Farley, whose encouragement led to the Christus/Mercy lectures being offered to a wider public, and to Christopher Bellitto of Paulist Press who patiently steered them as essays to final publication. Mr. Edward Schone earned special thanks for his superb manuscript management.

Most of all I thank the authors for surpassing our expectations. Their continuing cooperation made the entire project a joy.

Magdala Thompson

1.

Feminist Theology: The Heart of the Matter

Mary Aquin O'Neill

Introduction

It is my enviable task to inaugurate a series of theological reflections from a feminist perspective. Part of the challenge is to introduce the notion of feminist theology.

Conscious that neither the original audience nor the current readership necessarily shares the same faith or is at the same level of understanding of the topic, I want to be straightforward about the perspective from which this introduction is given.

Feminism is affecting nearly every religious tradition, and so it will affect the theology of that tradition, if there is one. To be clear, this introduction will deal only with the

1

impact of feminism on Christian theology. Even at that, it is important to note differences in that realm.

Roman Catholic theology has been dominated, until very recently, by priests—celibate men who do not live in day-to-day intimacy with women. Moreover, their training and education takes place, for the most part, in single-sex institutions where there is rarely a woman present to challenge what they think and say about the "opposite sex." This can lead to an idealization or to a demonization of women, neither of which has much to do with the realities of women and our lives.

Protestant theologians, for the most part married, are far less likely to fall into that particular trap, which is not to say that Protestant male thinkers are free of sexism. It is, rather, that sexism in the Protestant community takes a different form. Protestant reformers, in their zeal to restore Jesus to a central place in the piety of the people, downplayed the significance of Mary, the Mother of God, to the point where she has all but disappeared from the devotional life of mainline Protestants. (The high Anglican tradition, which is clearly different, is an exception.)

Roman Catholicism, by contrast, preserves in dogma and in liturgy an important place for this daughter of God. As a result, the search for the feminine archetype, the quest for the mother, that is going on in Christianity today will have a different starting point and a different configuration in the two traditions. While the viewpoints presented here are intended to be widely applicable, it is simply not possible to operate as if one were a theologian without tradition and perspective on these issues.

Already, we can identify a defining characteristic at the "heart" of feminist theology: a desire to include in consideration the reader and the author in addition to the content being conveyed; and an awareness that the material under consideration strikes deep wells of emotion. Simply put, one cannot, or at least should not, claim to have *the* perspective, but can only present *a* perspective, and hope it will lead to thoughtful consideration and an open dialogue with those who see things differently.

In this essay, I first explain what I understand the term "feminist theology" to mean. Then I indicate the extent to which the resulting perspective requires a revision of Christian theology. Next, I explain some of the shifts that have occurred in the use of sources and illustrate their importance for the interpretation of Jesus the Christ, an area of theology known as Christology. Finally, I try to summarize what I see to be at the heart of this development in Christian theology.

Feminist Theology

John Ciardi,[1] the poet, once wrote that "a man is what he does with his attention." It is a great truth, widely applicable.

In the early 1960s, it was customary, even in all-girl high schools, to sing at liturgy and at prayer services a hymn whose opening line goes, "Sons of God, hear his holy word, gather round the table of the Lord...."

In the '70s, a professor at a major university addressed a class of young men and women about to graduate and begin teaching careers. The professor's assignment was to give the students tips on successful teaching. The first tip he gave was to wear a different tie every day.

In the summer of 1995, Burger King ran an advertisement that capitalized on the success of the movie, *Pocahontas*. The voice-over said, "Ever since Pocahontas came to the big screen, every kid wants to be John Smith."

What do these three examples have in common? If you realize that each of them defines a reality solely on the basis of male experience, something has widened your attention. If you see that the girls and women in the audience are not being taken into account, in fact are being subtly defined out of the experience, something has sharpened your attention. You are now able to attend to what is not there, to feel with those who are being left out (and for women, that is an extremely important move, for what is being left out is our very selves).

This is indeed the heart of the matter.

I could paraphrase John Ciardi's quote, then, to say that a theology is what it does with its attention. A theology that is at once Christian and feminist would therefore be a theology done with an inclusive attention, a theology done with women in mind, a theology informed by the mind, heart, and imagination of women as well as of men.

4

Let me put it another way. The classic definition of theology is that it is faith seeking understanding.[2]

Feminist thinking challenges Christian theology to examine both parts of that definition: We must look—with the eyes of women—at what we have been taught to believe and at the way that we have been taught to understand. And then theology and theologians must make room in all the many houses for the truths and the ways of women.

This kind of looking and making room will require self-denial, not only on the part of men but on the part of women who are now convinced that the way men have done things is the only valuable way. Since the attention has been on men and their ways for so long, it will be painful to correct. A change of attention is not an easy experience. The gospel calls it *metanoia*—a transformation so total that nothing is ever the same again. The inclusion of women in Christian theology will result in no less a transformation.

Despite the popularity of the term, "feminist" is not an entirely satisfying name for the theology being described (and advocated) here. What I intend is not a subset of theology; it is not a field or a specialty that can be separated from other theological concerns. Inasmuch as all the theology we have inherited has been shaped by an exclusive attention, it will have to be revised. An exclusive attention is an attention that thinks only of the male when speaking about God or about humanity. It is an attention that assumes that whatever is said in this way applies equally to women or, worse, assumes that women are simply ruled out of some dimensions of the Christian life. Inasmuch as this is true, all of theology must be revised.

Other authors will address the reverberations of this inclusive attention on an understanding of God and on our ethical traditions. In consideration of that, I will demonstrate how this inclusive attention is affecting the way theologians approach the New Testament and what difference it can make to an understanding of Jesus the Christ.

The Sources

Men and women alike recognize Matthew, Mark, Luke, John, James, Peter, Andrew, Judas, Paul, Timothy, and Titus as some of the most important men of the New Testament. But what about Mary, Martha, Tabitha, Rhoda, Lois, Eunice, Lydia, Phoebe, Tryphaena, Tryphosa, Persis, Junia, and Chloe? Are they as well known as Salome, the woman taken in adultery, the Samaritan woman? Even Mary of Magdala, once known as the "apostle to the apostles," has come down to us mainly as a repentant prostitute rather than the fearless messenger of the good news of the resurrection. Peter sinned, too, but the Christian imagination never let his sin define him. It seems that the fallen women are more familiar to vast numbers of Christians than the female leaders.

It is true that, except for Mary, the Mother of Jesus, and Mary and Martha, there are few real stories connected with the women I listed just now. They are simply named by Paul and the author of the Acts of the Apostles, who thank these women for holding the church together by leadership, financial support, prayer, and suffering. On the other hand, many of the great stories in the New Testament fail to name the women involved: not only the Samaritan woman, but the Syro-Phoenician woman, the woman with a hemorrhage, the woman who anointed Jesus with precious nard are all nameless.

Women scholars, directing our attention to the foundational texts of the Christian religion, have detected these problems and others, not only with the way the stories have been interpreted, but also with the way the stories were written down. This is what scholars mean by the claim that an androcentric bias has shaped the source texts of Christianity. In simple terms, it means that what got written down was what seemed important to the writers and editors, all of whom—as far as we know—were men.

It does not mean, however, that women who study the New Testament have despaired of learning about the power of the gospel's call to women. Some extremely creative work is issuing from this very matrix of belief and suspicion. Following are two illustrations.

In an extended interpretation of the story of the woman at the well (John 4:1–42), Sandra Schneiders generates insights that enable us to see this woman—and women—anew.[3]

Schneiders reminds us that the encounter takes place at a well, a scenario full of meaning for anyone familiar with the Old Testament. Isaac's wife Rebecca, Jacob's beloved Rachel, and Moses' spouse Zipporah—all of them were discovered at a well. Schneiders interprets the gospel story in that light, showing the marital imagery that abounds in the scene: well, water, vessel, fruitful fields, sowing and reaping, and so on. For Schneiders, this is a story of the Jesus who woos back to the true God the one who has indeed had five husbands and now has none—the Samaritan people. In and through his exchange with this one woman—an exchange that is remarkable for the freedom the woman displays in challenging and responding to him—Jesus gains access to a Samaria that is "white for the harvest." His agent is the woman who, after making much over the water that draws her to the well daily, leaves her jug and runs off to tell her people about the man who has revealed so much to her. Schneiders opens our eyes to the meaning of the water jug, a staple of a woman's life. She writes, "Like the apostle—disciples in the synoptic gospels whose leaving of nets, boats, parents, or tax stall symbolized their abandonment of ordinary life to follow Jesus and become apostles, this woman abandons her daily concerns and goes off to evangelize the town."[4]

Moreover, the Samaritan woman's efforts are immediately effective, for according to Schneiders, "this woman is the first and only person (presented) in the public life of Jesus through whose word of witness a group of people is brought to 'come and see' and 'to believe in Jesus.'"[5]

What about the image of Jesus in this story? Schneiders discloses how playful he is with the woman. There is a heterosexual dynamic going on in this text: a man relates to a woman. Each lets the other be who the other is, without trying to manipulate the other in any way. The woman has power and is not afraid to use it. Jesus does not try to stifle her. He accepts her challenges and answers them. Both are changed by the interaction: she leaves to be about something more important than drawing water; he is no longer hungry, and this mystifies his male disciples when they return.

What would our Christian world be like if male leaders related to intelligent, strong women as Jesus does in this story? What would it be like if strong, intelligent women were as playful and fair toward men as the Samaritan woman is? Surely the Samarias of our day would be more effectively evangelized.

A second example of an interpretation of revelation done with a feminist consciousness comes from the work of Hisako Kinukawa. Her book is called *Women and Jesus in Mark: A Japanese Feminist Perspective.*[6]

Seeing in first-century Palestine a culture not unlike her own, a "culture of shame," Kinukawa interprets the story of the hemorrhaging woman in Mark's Gospel. In this story she sees a woman move from outcast to volitional agent to challenger of the establishment. Most of all, she sees a woman who calls Jesus to be his true self.

Under the system in effect at the time, women were rendered unclean by their menstrual cycle, and anyone touching them would also be made unclean. If a bleeding woman were to touch a man without his knowledge, she could be put to death.

The woman in the story had been bleeding for twelve years. She had exhausted her money on doctors who did her no good, and she was now almost without hope. In her desperation, she conceived the scheme of touching the man about whom she had heard so much. Something told her that even to touch the hem of his garment would be enough to save her. And so it was, for the text tells us that as soon as she touched Jesus' cloak, she felt the bleeding stop and knew that she was changed. But Jesus felt something also: he knew that power had gone out from him. When Jesus cried out, "Who touched me?" the woman had a decision to make. She could hide her deed and hope not to be discovered, or she could come forward in peril of death. Risking everything, she thrust herself into the circle surrounding Jesus and threw herself at his feet. Now Jesus had to decide: follow the law and have her condemned, or respond to her faith and confirm her cure. "Daughter," he said, welcoming her back into the family, "your faith has made you well; go in peace and be healed of your disease." As Kinukawa observes, Jesus "does not attack the purity laws directly; he negates them by ignoring them."[7]

Yet it is the woman who took the initiative. "She challenges the boundary and makes Jesus become truly a savior."[8] The woman is saved, not just by being delivered from her physical condition but by being accepted as a member of the community as she is.

Seen with the eyes of a woman, this story is not just about the power of Jesus. It is about the power of a woman's faith to claim a cure, to risk dying for wholeness, to challenge the man of God to take a stand. It is also about a man of God who sides with the outcast, who welcomes her daring, who recognizes her faith. Understood in this way, it speaks directly to our times.

Christology

On the basis of these two stories, one can already see that new interpretations of familiar gospel stories change the way one understands Jesus. It is impossible to hold on to a notion that Jesus comes on the scene to change others but remains unaffected himself. These stories, and many others not recounted here, show Jesus in a relationship of reciprocity, of give and take, of initiative and response. It is not always Jesus who initiates; it is not always Jesus who has the last word. Inasmuch as our images of men and their roles in the church (and their images of themselves) have been modeled on Jesus, this new look at old texts should occasion a thorough rethinking of those images.

The image of Jesus inherited in the Catholic tradition, and probably in others as well, is of a man who needs nothing from others. He appears fully formed, having it all together. During his public life, he takes charge of situations, has the answers, knows what to do, sends forth power, and—when he experiences anything like fatigue or a depression of spirit—he withdraws from people and communes with his heavenly father. Doesn't this sound amazingly like the ideal priest? Perhaps even the ideal father? Clearly, there is evidence to the contrary. Lazarus was Jesus' close friend—so close Jesus wept when hearing that Lazarus had died. Jesus spent time at the home of Lazarus, with the sisters Mary and Martha. Apparently, Jesus so enjoyed communing with Mary that he rejected Martha's attempt to take her away to the kitchen. But this is not the picture of Jesus that has dominated the Christian imagination.

We are only beginning to see how deeply our notions of heroism have shaped our understanding and expectations of Jesus, and vice versa. Can we let the goodness of our own humanity reshape notions of both heroism and Christology? I think of the interview that the actor Christopher Reeve granted Barbara Walters, ABC correspondent, after a disabling accident that left him, who once played the role of Superman, nearly completely paralyzed. The courage he displayed from his motorized chair, the reflections he gave on coming to accept the help of others, especially his wife, raise profound questions about our humanity. Who is the real superman? Is this man lesser or greater now that he acknowledges and embraces his need for others—now that he allows others to care for him?

There is another truth buried in the traditions of the gospels, one that can only be seen when one takes a developmental angle. This is an angle at which women are particularly adept, as Sally Cuneen shows throughout her excellent work, *Mother Church: What the Experience of Women Is Teaching Her.*[9] Women are adept at it because for so long the responsibility of dealing with the developing person has been relegated to us. The developmental angle can occasion an important shift. One moves from thinking of Jesus as fully developed from the time he left the womb to thinking of the real implications of the confession that he is truly human. In doing so, one comes to realize that he not only grew in wisdom, age, and grace, but he did so first under the guidance of parents and then, as is true of us all, in living interaction with others.

Christology influenced by women, then, discloses the becoming of Jesus. In this regard, consider the example of the wedding feast of Cana. When Mary says, "They have no wine," Jesus retorts, "Woman, what is that to you and me?" I learned a great lesson when I asked a class of undergraduates why they thought Jesus answered his mother so sharply. One young man said, "Maybe he felt she was urging him into his growing up time and he didn't feel ready."

The excitement of this answer, as with all answers that come from deep within the person, is that the young man was relating to Jesus. The student imagined that, in order to respond to what his mother had pointed out, Jesus would have to leave childhood behind. There followed in that class an extended conversation about the role the mother played in Jesus' life and in the lives of the students. They—especially the young men—indicated that the belief of the mother and later of the women in their lives could help them overcome childishness and attempt things that they did not yet feel ready for. At the same time, others—especially the young women—saw that however Mary got Jesus to change his mind (and this is the way they read the story), she did so with grace and subtlety, not by making a scene and embarrassing him.

This leads to a final point about Christology. Feminist and other liberationist theologians have discovered that Jesus came to a way of relating to women, to the poor, to the outcast that was remarkably free from the prejudices and inequities dictated by law and custom. But until very recently, there was little reflection on the human experiences that might have brought him to this way of relating. Now, however, with the marvelous resources provided by those who are studying childrearing and its influence on the developing person, theologians are in a position to make a new connection between Jesus, in whom the character of God is revealed, and the parents who taught, protected, and molded him. Joseph, let us remember, is described with the awesome epithet "just man." He who had every right to reject Mary and see her punished to the full extent of the law was not bent on doing that at all, but sought a way to be faithful to the law without hurting this one who was carrying a child not his own. The message of the angel delivers Joseph from his quandary, but not before we have had a chance to see the character of the man: he is law abiding but not vengeful, loving but not unmindful of the constraints of tradition and society. Once he is convinced of God's will, however, law, tradition, and society's expectations count for little. He is above all a man of God.

More is known of Mary. There is the dialogue of the annunciation, in which she relates to the messenger of God in a fashion not unlike the Samaritan woman: asking questions, puzzling out answers, deciding to respond to an invitation that will alter the course of her life. There are the words of Mary's Magnificat sounding a clarion call for the poor, the downtrodden, the hungry. There is the example of her behavior at the wedding feast, where food and drink were important enough that she noticed and acted. There is the wordless witness of her standing at the foot of the cross.

If Jesus could be challenged by women, was attentive to the poor, taught a way of justice that did not preclude mercy, accorded respect to those that others despised, surely the seeds of that development were sown in his home and nurtured by his parents. A developmental angle on Christology could well serve to refocus attention on the grandeur of the parental vocation and on the mystery of childbearing and childrearing.

Thus an inclusive theology sees connections where they have been ignored or denied, for the theology that feminists seek to shape is a relational, holistic theology that does not divorce the man from the child, public action from the private life, the divine from the deeply human.

Central to this theology is the determination to hold together what has previously been separated, if not dichotomized. The content of theology—the deposit of faith as it is often called—cannot be apprehended apart from attention to the audience and to the interpreter. Each of us exists as limitation and openness; none of us has a comprehensive viewpoint that would enable us to say we need no help in coming to understand what we believe. This is painfully and especially true where the content concerns women and men. For too long, men have been sure that what they say about being human applies to all: yet we are not all sons of God, some of us are daughters; we do not all wear a tie, some of us wear scarves and bows; we do not all want to be John Smith, some of us want to be Pocahontas.

Conclusion

If men are willing to listen to women, to receive insights that women have to give, it will be a new day for theology. Some of the insights I have highlighted in this essay are summarized as follows.

1. Women bring to theology a consciousness of the ways in which women have been misrepresented or positively ruled out by traditional Christian theology. It will not do for men to deny this. Accepting it means that men as well as women must learn to approach sacred texts with a mixture of faith and suspicion.

2. It is the responsibility of women theologians to read the Christian traditions from the distaff side, with the eyes of women, and to find therein good news for women and for men.

3. Insofar as a Christian view of things begins with the New Testament revelation, it is imperative to interpret Jesus and his ways. Jesus' way is the paradigmatic Christian way. Therefore, his manner of relating to the Samaritan woman and the woman with the hemorrhage, and their way of relating to him, should be the model for relationships between Christian men and women. It is a relationship characterized by respect and an alternating initiative and response. It results in mutual transformation.

4. Women have as much right as men in the new dispensation to take risks for the sake of our own health and salvation. We, too, must judge the value of the law in the face of desperate situations and failed solutions.

5. Caring for the developing human being is not only as important as relating to the (imagined) fully mature person, but it gives one resources for theology that have long been overlooked and at times ridiculed. Parenting, then, is an indispensable source for theological knowledge, and Christian theology needs to respect that fact.

6. The truths revealed by God are received not only by the works of analysis and reason, but also by way of emotion and imagination. These capabilities are not sex linked; they are deeply human ways to know and each way is open to both sexes.

7. Faith seeking understanding requires both heart and head. The effort to defend and to recover those elements of Christian faith that speak to the loyalties and intelligence of women may well open the hearts and minds of all.[10]

Notes

1. Line remembered from a poetry reading.
2. Attributed to Anselm of Canterbury (1033–1109).
3. See Sandra Schneiders, *The Revelatory Text: Interpreting the New Testament as Sacred Scripture* (San Francisco: HarperSanFrancisco, 1991), chap. 7, 180–200.
4. Ibid., 192.
5. Ibid., 193.
6. Hisako Kinukawa, *Women and Jesus in Mark: A Japanese Feminist Perspective* (Maryknoll, NY: Orbis, 1994).
7. Ibid., 46.

8. Ibid., 47.
9. Sally Cuneen, *Mother Church: What the Experience of Women Is Teaching Her* (New York: Paulist Press, 1991).
10. I am grateful to Heidi Hansan for the editorial suggestions that enabled me to transform what was originally a talk into what is now an essay without losing voice or content.

2.

Feminism and Hope

Margaret A. Farley

Theological hope as both an attitude and a virtue has been integral to the Christian tradition. Concerns about anchoring this hope and nurturing it have been central to Christian spirituality. Christian women, as well as men, have lived in hope; they have tried to share their hopes; they have "hoped against hope" for themselves and those they love. Yet Christian and post-Christian feminists have been critical of traditional understandings and functions of Christian hope, just as they have found it necessary to critique traditional formulations of nearly every key doctrinal formulation of faith. My purpose in this essay is to consider carefully the feminist critique of Christian theological hope and to propose a feminist retrieval and reconstruction of a theology of hope.[1]

Preliminary Clarifications

Let me begin with two clarifications that will help to shape what I say about feminism and hope. First, I want to indicate what it is that I mean when I use the term "feminism." This is, of course, a contested term—even among feminists; and among those who oppose feminism, it is almost always seriously misunderstood. Moreover, there are many feminisms; that is, feminism today appears in significantly diverse forms. What I mean by it here, therefore, is simply this: Feminism is a position (a belief and a movement) that is opposed to discrimination on the basis of gender.[2] It is therefore opposed to sexism in all of its forms, including institutional structures and practices that are discriminatory (such as gendered role differentiations). Since sexism has been and remains pervasively discriminatory against women, feminism opposes women's unequal access to goods and services, and it struggles to eliminate barriers to women's participation in decision making in church and society. Feminism is also opposed, therefore, to ideologies, beliefs, attitudes, and behaviors that establish or reinforce these discriminating structures, systems, and practices. In addition, it is opposed to other forms of unjust discrimination and patterns of domination; it includes in its analysis the socially constructed connections among gender, race, class, as well as age, sexual orientation, and other characteristics that can be the basis of discrimination and oppression.

21

Margaret A. Farley

Positively, the form of feminism that I am describing seeks to bring about equality and concrete well-being for women and men in all spheres of human life, interpersonal and institutional. It is not anti-men, but it is necessarily pro-women (precisely because, as I have already indicated, gender discrimination remains largely against women). Feminism therefore incorporates a strategic bias for women. It is, however, ultimately pro-human, for it affirms the fundamental claim of all persons to respect as persons who are characterized as having basic needs, a capacity for freedom, and deep desires for fulfillment.

Given this meaning of *feminism,* there are nonetheless many forms that feminism now takes—diverse theories and theologies, even diverse feminist ethics. I do not attempt to sort these out here, but my rendering of feminist critiques of Christian theological hope, as well as my effort to provide a reconstruction, will give some indication of the diversity of feminist perspectives.

The second clarification I want to make relates to the starting point for feminist theology and ethics—and therefore the starting point for a feminist theology of hope. Feminist theologies generally appeal to the standard sources for Christian theology—that is, sacred scripture, tradition, other (secular) disciplines of human knowledge, and contemporary experience. What is unique about feminist theology, however, is that it begins (like all feminist theory) with women's experience. We can expect, then, that both the critique of traditional ideas about Christian hope, and

22

responses to this critique, will begin with women's experience—diverse, yet in some ways shared.

What are the experiences of women that constitute the "social location" in which the word of God's revelation must be heard if this word is to be a source of life and hope for women? Women know them well, because they include all of the experiences of women's lives—in families, churches, societies. But feminist theology begins most specifically with women's shared experience of struggle—against poverty, exploitation, marginalization, domination, repression, and oppression. The stories of women worldwide are stories of the struggle for liberation from racism, unjust family structures, sexual abuse. They are stories of the failure of educational systems to take women seriously, the refusal of religious traditions to acknowledge the full humanity of women, the rejection of women whose sexual orientation does not fit the conventional expectations of church and society, and the marginalization of women through unyielding interpretations of secular and sacred traditions.

Women do not, in and through such experiences, see themselves only as victims, without any strength or without possibilities for fullness of life. Nor do women interpret their lives (except in the most dire situations) as without joy and achievement and beauty. Nevertheless, until there is a home in this world for all—women, children, and men; until the world awakens to the plight of massive numbers of women with AIDS (especially in developing nations); until attention is paid to the rape of women as a strategy of war; until religious traditions recognize that the faith of all is stifled as long as women are excluded from roles of leadership, the work of feminist theology must go on. In particular, Christian feminist theologies must continue to critique interpretations of divine revelation and formulations of Christian faith that serve to perpetuate these kinds of situations. Feminist theologians must continue to re-interpret their traditions—to retrieve lost treasures and forge better insights—until these traditions offer genuinely "good news" for women everywhere.

The Critique

What, then, is the problem with Christian understandings of hope? Why do feminists find Christian theologies of hope inadequate, even harmful, to women? No one—least of all feminist theologians—argues that women (or men) ought not to hope. No feminist analysis aims at taking hope away from women. Indeed, feminism as a movement has represented women's efforts to take hold of their lives and move them forward in hope and hopefulness. Years ago, Doris Lessing placed a line on the frontispiece of one of her novels, in the voice of a woman: "I am so tired of it; and also tired of the future before it comes."[3] It was against this experience of weariness and despair that women mobilized, in many generations, first to reflect on their reasons for hope, and then to awaken hope as a sustainer of their actions for justice—for themselves and their children. Feminist critiques of a Christian construal of hope parallel in many respects the critique of religion promoted by key modern theorists. That is, like Marx, Nietzsche, and Freud, some feminists have argued that Christian hope has all too often been "pie in the sky hope"—a hope in another world that makes people passive and all too patient in the face of injustice and oppression in this world. Suffering and death, they say, have been romanticized by Christian teachers and preachers, as a holy way to reach a world beyond. Feminist (now post-Christian) Mary Daly, therefore, joined Nietzsche in declaring Christianity a religion for victims, a religion that obsessed about pain and death and that made submission rather than resistance a virtue—especially for women.[4] Religious hope, agreed other feminists, gives a false sense that all is really well, and "all shall be well." Belief in an ultimate future, in this view, short-circuits commitment to a proximate future. Desires are thus restrained (repressed), and they become only wishful thinking. The moral demand to alleviate situations of oppression goes therefore unheeded.

Some feminists have noted, further, that this kind of hope works especially against women. It has a gendered face. That is, cultures have frequently conditioned women more than men to passivity; and though this can be a courageous and in some ways noble passivity of endurance, it nonetheless remains drastically ineffective in the face of tragedy. When, contrary to this, women have been active in resisting the causes of the suffering of their children, a resigned hope has nonetheless characterized their response to their own burdens and powerlessness.

Of course, many Christian women do not recognize this as a description of their present experience. These women do not shy away from strong active involvements in movements for justice around the world. But then, many of them also do not think much about hope in a world other than this one, nor have the young among them, as women, yet encountered the kinds of burdens, limitations, relentless exploitation that may yet await them insofar as they take this world as their primary and even sole concern. Christian feminists generally have developed an eschatology that is resolutely this-worldly, aiming to correct any bias toward another world and refusing to be deflected from the moral imperatives that confront our time.[5]

The feminist critique of traditional notions of hope goes even deeper, however. It reaches, for example, to the charge that Christian hope, based as it is on the death and resurrection of Jesus, is in essence a denial of finitude. Post-Christian Carol Christ argues that Christian hope therefore constitutes a failure to affirm "this life on this earth, in these bodies."[6] While we need not absolutely rule out the possibility of life after death, Christ says, we ought not to live here in the light of it. Hope in another life should above all not prevent women from recognizing their real home in this world and affirming precisely here their power and potential for action. This is more than a call to resist injustices. It is an assertion that one should in every way "forget" a future that is unlimited and place one's energies and hopes in what can be accomplished here in the world of our experience.

More than this, Christian feminists like Rosemary Radford Ruether argue that unless we are willing to focus on this world we will not attend to the vulnerable ecological future of the Earth.[7] Hope in an unending future for ourselves can obscure our present responsibilities for the survival of this planet and the well-being of the universe. In this view, hope for an end to this world, and ultimate happiness in a world beyond, is a form of self-preoccupation that needs to be transcended or broken. This means that belief in personal immortality must, at least in principle, be relinquished. Only thus will we succeed in the kind of de-centering of ourselves that is necessary for the future of the whole of creation. Surrender to the possible loss of our own selves in this sense[8] will empower us to attend to creation as we know it, and to care for all who participate and dwell therein. The call, therefore, is to go beyond what are sometimes called "male models" of individual autonomy, desire for continuity of personal identity, and obsession with one's own absolute future.[9]

These are some of the critiques that feminists offer of traditional understandings of Christian hope. The critiques are salutary, whatever our final judgment of their validity. We may, however, need more than this from feminist theology if the hope of Christians, especially Christian women, is to be renewed. To some extent, the problem with Christian hope is whether hope is only of things "unseen,"[10] or whether it also "sees," in some way, the object of its hope; whether hope is only for the future, or whether it also commits us to the present; whether to hope implies—or leads to—powerlessness or power. Let me turn, then, to a feminist response to these critiques—to a feminist retrieval and reconstruction of elements deep in the Christian tradition.

A Response

Before we can consider a response and revision, we need to ask what there is about hope that makes all of this so important. Why should this be a concern for feminists or anyone else? A clue lies in our manifest *need* of hope—of belief in a future, if you will. For better or for worse, human persons are the kind of beings who cannot live without a sense of a future. Our lives are lived not all-at-once. They are stretched out in time. Being alive for us includes, requires, an experience of past and present moving into a future. When we experience our lives as futureless (closed, stifled, stopped), we find them intolerable. "Hope is for the soul what breathing is for the living organism," wrote Gabriel Marcel.[12] Simply to be alive is for us to experience the desire and need for more life—just as to love is to experience the desire and need for fuller union, greater affirmation of the beloved, and an extended future for the love. Hence, hope may appear in the form of trust, belief, hope that the deep relationships that are the fabric of our lives and the structure of our hearts will last forever; that they can live into an unlimited future. Creation in us groans—not just in travail of evil and pain but in yearning for fullness of life.[13] If, with Carol Christ and others, we accept a finitude that needs no life after death, then consent to our death is precisely consent to a final limit to our personal future, not only for ourselves but for our relationships.[14] We need hope, then, because of who and what we are. We need hope lest we despair of life and love itself.

Insofar as our present is marked by suffering—whether our own or that of those we love—hope takes the form of believing that things will change, that there is a future, immediate or remote, when something of the suffering will change.[15] The opposite of "pie in the sky" illusion is not despair of any new possibility. To hope is to believe that what looks like a closed and settled fate is not really so. Without some hope we are crushed. We wither and die even while we live. Without hope in a change that can lessen suffering, or alter its meaning, or provide us with the strength to resist it or bear it or move us beyond it, we ourselves are forced to make another kind of change. We capitulate to despair, perhaps cursing God (or all reality), perhaps seeing the world as a drama of absurdity that needs no change because it is meaningless in any case. Or perhaps we settle for what others tell us *is* our life, but that leads to our premature death.

Nonetheless, once again, we need hope because we are alive, and we experience our lives as needing, desiring, a future. Christian hope is part of human hope in this sense. But it also transforms human hope, not only grounding it and strengthening it but giving it a different future. But what can be said about Christian hope from a feminist perspective, chastened as we must be by a feminist critique?

Margaret A. Farley

My own proposal is that Christian hope need not give up hope in "another world" where lies what as yet "eye hath not seen nor ear heard."[16] Christian hope must, however, include also hope for this present world. The key to all of this is twofold. It includes the connection between these worlds and the requirement of our commitment to one another in the course of our life together. We have important clues to this connection and to the nature of the commitment required.

The most crucial clue is to be found in a feminist interpretation of God's relationship to us and the connection between this and our relationship to one another. Elizabeth Johnson argues that language about the triune God, spoken from a feminist theological perspective, illuminates central elements in classical trinitarian doctrine. It places in relief the radical equality, mutuality, and community that characterize God's life. This in turn offers us the "ultimate paradigm" for our own personal and social lives.[17] Johnson does not pursue the paradigm in relation to the questions of human hope I am addressing here. But it nonetheless offers insight for these questions precisely because it sheds light on the connections between another world and this one. As such, it may provide us with a theological warrant for hope (in this world and the next), and it may guide our action in accordance with this hope.

Think, for example, of our questions of theological hope in the light of the Gospel of John 15:9–12. Despite John's apparent limitations in understanding inclusive community, chapter after chapter of this Gospel records Jesus'

30

view not only of a model of being but a model of loving and acting.[18] Climaxing in chapter 15, we are given the words of Jesus, "As God has loved me, so I have loved you," and, "As I have loved you, so you are to love one another." "As God has loved me, or in other words, *as love flows in the life of God's own self,* so I love you and you must love one another." But how does love flow in the life of God? This is a life and a love of infinitely receptive activity and infinitely active receptivity; a love and a life of utter equality and mutuality, consummate giving and receiving, distinguishable yet one in a life of perfect communion.

It is this, Jesus says, this life and love that provide the *model according to which God also loves us.* "As God loves me, so I have loved you." A self-emptying God raises up the beloved and offers to all a share in the fullness of God's life. But there is more: this model becomes in turn the *model required for our relationships with one another* "This is my commandment, that you love one another as I have loved you." A model, a graced possibility, and a command are signified together.

Nothing, then, is as we might have assumed; business is not "as usual" in the sociological unfolding of our roles and relationships. We are not given a pattern of superiority and subordination; we are not told of a dominating God who exacts submission from a people; we have not here a model in which men are to be superior to women, clergy to laity, pastors to congregations, teachers to students, one nation or race to another. In all human relationships, equality and mutuality are to be at least the goal, if not yet a completely applicable ethical norm. Even relationships that must be unequal for a time (as between parents and children) have as their ultimate fulfillment a friendship between equals.

This is a model for this world, but embedded in it is a revelation of our possible future. No more radical goal is imaginable for us than the goal of universal communion—each of us with God and with one another in God. We have in Jesus' portrayal of his life and ours a news so "good" that it is difficult to believe. We have a proclamation and a promise, a command and a gift; and it stretches from this world to another.

What I am trying to say here, then, is that our understandings of Christian hope (a hope that need not leave us diminished or disempowered for action or without insight into the form our own actions should take) should be lodged in our understandings of God's own life and of God's relationship to us—in the connection between God's life and ours. And in this, there is to be found a connection between the present and the future, between "another" world and this one.

Let me try to unfold this in three steps: First, the ground of Christian hope is God's promise and God's action toward us. Second, this promise and this action turn us to this world and not only a world beyond. And third, there is nonetheless continuity between this world and the next.

1. *First, then, the ground of Christian hope is God's promise and God's action toward us.* Theological hope is, after all, hope not ultimately in human individuals, or

human institutions, governments, churches or even movements, but in God. It is, of course, not unconnected with hope for persons, things, activities, efforts, and social arrangements in this world. It is hope in God for us—and for those we love. If we are criticized for wishful thinking about an unlimited future, or for simply projecting what we want to be true into an illusory hope, how can we respond? Perhaps our only response is to look to the promises of God in relation to which we take our stand. The biblical record of God's word to us—in both the First and Second Testaments—is filled with promises that our sufferings will be healed and that longings will be fulfilled. Here is recorded again and again the promise that things can change.

In a deep sense, our hope remains in things as yet "unseen." There is no other assurance for us than what we can find in a revealed word. There is no other way to receive this assurance than by trusting this word, throwing our lot with it, letting go our objections in order to experience its presence. Ours is a hope for a future that is not yet realized. And yet, and yet, what is revealed in the promise is what is "already," along with "not yet"; what is made possible through this revelation is that we can "see" as well as "not see" the object of our hope. Take as a key example what is revealed to us in and through the cross of Jesus Christ. There are those who say (some feminists among them) that the cross, central to Christian faith, signals Christianity's preoccupation with suffering and death. The cross cuts off our energy and our urgency for action regarding what can be hoped for here and now. But those who say this are wrong. The meaning of the cross is precisely *not* death, but rather, that a *relationship holds*. No matter what the forces of evil can do to break the bonds of love, a relationship can hold. And it is this relationship that becomes our life—already present, historically accomplished.

The relationship holds even in the face of death, for death no longer has the last word. Christianity has as its center not death but life. We can know our own possibility of death—of the many ways of laying down our lives or having them taken from us; but we can also know our own possibilities of resurrection.

Hope, therefore, is *not* always and only of things completely unseen. In our experience there are connections between what we see and cannot see, what we feel and cannot touch, what we hear and what is still silent. We are at times given an inkling that the joy we need and yearn for, the justice and peace, freedom and wholeness, are not afterthoughts on God's part; that though there is discontinuity between our lives of mourning and the life for which we hope, there is also continuity. Sometimes, at least, "our hearts are burning" as we recognize God's presence, as we feel the surge of life within us, and glimpse the horizon of an approaching future. God's promise and action in and toward us is "already," even though there is more that is surely "not yet."

2. *God's promise and action turn us to this world and not only to a world beyond.* The biblical record of God's word to us is filled with promises, but it is also filled with calls, even imperatives, to change some things now. It is, then, simply wrong to think that we are merely to wait patiently, passively, without resistance or hard work or risk of almost everything in order to bring change. It is also not adequate to think that the ideal of Christian love is to live and work as if we did not hope that our work will make a difference. God does not play games with us. Our labor is not some kind of test for us, in response to some rules of some game.

Feminist (and other) critics are right to charge that Christianity in some of its developments has been too "other-worldly." Overall, however, Christianity cannot be said to be a world-denying religion. Whatever the importance of "other worlds," the Christian tradition has incorporated key beliefs and insights that should continually counter tendencies of apathy toward this world—toward its possibilities and its needs. Christianity, for example, has affirmed (though not always without some difficulty) the importance of human desire—not only for God, but for the world as bearer of revelation, embodiment of beauty, a place where God dwells. The problem with loving the world is loving it well—neither exploiting it nor encouraging domination of some peoples over others; not fleeing it, without giving our lives to mend it, to liberate its peoples, to be true to ourselves. Christian hope is not mere resignation, nor is our task to "swoon in the shadow"[19] of the cross when we should be laboring in its light.

Though death will come, it is not only not the last word; it does not undo the importance of life in this world. Though "in the twinkling of an eye" everything can change (God can come quickly, and sorrows can pass away), it makes a difference what we do in the meantime. If our goal is communion, and we are called to walk along the way to that goal, then it matters more, not less, that we begin and sustain relationships of justice and friendship here and now; that we protect bodies and ease spirits; that we rear our young wisely and care for those who are old; and that we awaken to the needs and possibilities of our near neighbors and far.

Since our lives together are embodied in this world, we shall not ultimately leave it behind for a disembodied communion. The world around us, and not only ourselves, will be transformed as a whole, as our home forever. Or at least this is theologically plausible—enough so that we need not sacrifice personal identity in order to see our profound obligations to the world as a whole. Our need to de-center ourselves in order to love the whole of creation does not require, nor will it be secured by, abandonment of our hope in personal immortality or the unlimited future of those we love. If the communion to which we are called is with God and with all others in God, then all is at the center,[20] if we let our hearts see it so. Whatever the discontinuity between this world and another, there is a profound continuity between what we begin here, do here, and its fulfillment in an unlimited future.

3. *This brings me to my third and final step in trying to unfold a Christian and a feminist understanding of hope. It brings me to my claim that there is continuity between this world and the next.* If it is a mistake to hope in another world but not in this one, it is also a mistake to hope only in this world and not in another—especially if the "other" world is finally one with this world transformed. "As God has loved me, so I have loved you." "As I have loved you, so you are to love one another." This is the starting point. This is the goal. This is to be our one life, for now and forever. How we live it now makes "all the difference in the world" for its ultimate future—not because we earn a future reward, but because what we do now is constitutive of the future. And that there is a future makes "all the difference in the world" for the present.

Feminist theologians and ethicists have argued that we must be willing to stand in solidarity with the marginalized and be willing to take concrete actions for change. They have insisted that we must search for a "usable past" for women (in our experiences and in our traditions), and that we must project a future that learns from the underside of history. Feminists have argued further that we need to understand a "usable future" in order to interpret the past and the present, in order to direct our actions in the light of God's promises and God's presence.

Margaret A. Farley

Whether we are trying to interpret (and liberate) our traditions or transform our social structures, we can "think from the other end,"[21] which is revealed and experienced in "inklings" of what will be. In so doing, we sharpen our obligation to build community in which none are isolated, to struggle for justice with everyone poor or oppressed, to heal the multiple forms of human suffering, and to assist in the release and nurture of life so abundant that not even death can stop it.

Theological hope, then, is hope in God, for all of us. It relies on the relationship between God's love and our own, on the connection between our own actions and God's promise, and on the continuity between this world and the next. It is a hope accessible and intelligible to feminists and all Christians. I end with Jesus' words to the women who followed him to his death: "Daughters of Jerusalem, weep not for me but for yourselves and your children."[22] Jesus recognized that women know at least two kinds of tears: tears of desolation, which when they have all been shed, leave the well dry, and tears of consolation, which water our hearts and give us strength, and then water us all the way to the sea of action.[23] These latter are the tears of hope.

Notes

1. This essay incorporates but revises and greatly expands upon some sections of my "Feminist Theology and Ethics: The Contributions of Elizabeth A. Johnson," in *Things New and*

Old, ed. Phyllis Zagano and Terrence W. Tilley (New York: Crossroad, 1999), 1–19.

2. For a fuller rendering of this, see my article, "Feminist Ethics," in *Feminist Ethics and the Catholic Moral Tradition*, ed. C. Curran, M. Farley, and R. McCormick (New York: Paulist Press, 1996), 5–10. This description of feminism is admittedly more "liberal" than other descriptions might be.

3. Lessing attributes this quotation to Olive Schreiner. See Doris Lessing, *Martha Quest* (New York: Harper Collins, 1962), 1.

4. See Mary Daly, *Beyond God the Father: Toward a Philosophy of Women's Liberation* (Boston: Beacon Press, 1973), 70, 146.

5. This sort of eschatology characterizes, for example, the majority of the essays in *Liberating Eschatology*, ed. Margaret A. Farley and Serene Jones (Louisville, KY: Westminster John Knox Press, 1999).

6. Carol Christ, *Laughter of Aphrodite: Reflections on a Journey to the Goddess* (San Francisco: Harper & Row, 1987), 214.

7. Rosemary Radford Ruether, *Gaia and God: An Ecofeminist Theology of Earth Healing* (San Francisco: Harper Collins, 1992), 250–53.

8. This form of self-surrender is not to be confused with the denigration of the self that most feminists have resisted; that is, it is not to be confused with a willingness to be used as a mere means by and for others, a resignation to the role of a "doormat."

9. Ruether, *Gaia and God*, 253.

10. See, for example, Romans 8:24–25.

11. See my fuller treatment of these matters in *Personal Commitments: Beginning, Keeping, Changing* (San Francisco: Harper & Row, Publishers, 1986), chaps. 4–5; also in "Feminist Theology and Ethics," 16–17.

12. Gabriel Marcel, *Homo Viator*, trans. Emma Crauford (New York: Harper & Row, 1965), 10–11.

13. Romans 8:22–23.

14. This is why people—perhaps men more than women—have through the centuries in some cultures (not all), and even in our own, been concerned with genetically related offspring as a way to immortalize themselves. This may not be a hope in unlimited life, but it derives from it.
15. See my consideration of these same concerns in "Feminist Theology and Ethics," 16.
16. 1 Corinthians 2:9.
17. Elizabeth A. Johnson, *She Who Is: The Mystery of God in Feminist Theological Discourse* (New York: Crossroad, 1992), 222.
18. See my short review of this text in "Feminist Theology and Ethics," 6–7.
19. Teilhard de Chardin, cited in Christopher F. Mooney, *Teilhard de Chardin and the Mystery of Christ* (New York: Harper & Row, 1966), 119.
20. For a marvelous expansion of imagery in this regard, see C. S. Lewis, *Perelandra* (New York: Macmillan Company, 1944), 230–33.
21. See Letty N. Russell, *The Future of Partnership* (Philadelphia: Westminster Press, 1979), 51–53.
22. Luke 23:28.
23. This metaphor was first suggested to me by Beverly Gouaux, in a letter many years ago.

3.

Freedom, Emancipation, and Deliverance: Toward a Theology of Freedom

M. *Shawn Copeland*

Freedom, emancipation, deliverance: these are chief among the volatile and charged notions in that cluster of issues that has enthralled human reflection and action from biblical times to the present. The Hebrew Bible (what Christians call the Old Testament) testifies to the mighty deeds of a God who freed and emancipated a people, who delivered them from the hands of their Egyptian oppressors so that they might live and worship according to the covenant God would establish with them. For nearly 3,000 years, the ritual commemoration of Passover has chronicled the experience of the Hebrew peoples with slavery, brutality, and death, and with freedom, emancipation, and deliverance. The Haggadah encourages not only the memory of these events, but each Jew's personal identification with them: "In every generation let each man look upon himself as if *he* came forth out of Egypt."[1] Each year, then, the spiritual descendants of Abraham gather to drink wine; to eat roasted lamb, bitter herbs, and unleavened bread; to remember and to tell this story:

> A wandering Aramean was my father; and he went down into Egypt and sojourned there, few in number; and there he became a nation, great, mighty, and populous. And the Egyptians treated us harshly, and afflicted us, and laid upon us hard bondage. Then we cried to the Lord the God of our fathers, and the Lord heard our voice, and saw our affliction, our toil, and our oppression; and the Lord brought us out of Egypt with a mighty hand and an outstretched arm, with great terror, with signs and wonders; and brought us to this land, a land flowing with milk and honey. (Deut 26:5-10)

Freedom, emancipation, deliverance are recurring themes in the Hebrew Bible because what the people experience spiritually and socially is the saving mercy of the Lord God Adonai.

I

The ancient Greek philosophy of Plato and Aristotle accommodated freedom and slavery on the grounds that it was natural for some to be held in bondage or in slavery and others to be free or to be masters. Historian David Brion Davis argues that Plato "supplied the elements for a theory of intellectual inferiority as the natural basis for slavery." Plato maintained that "a slave might hold a true belief but could never know the truth of his belief, since he was inherently deficient in reason."[2]

Plato's philosophy not only accommodated slavery, it quartered Athenian contempt for women of the day, "categoriz[ing] them together with children and animals, with the immature, the sick and the weak."[3] And it is well to remember that no woman participates in person in any of the Socratic dialogues (although the high point of the discourse of the *Symposium* is said to come from the mouth of the priestess Diotima). Even in the *Republic,* with its daring inclusion of women among the ranks of the guardians, women are undermined. Before this revolutionary proposal is introduced

> it is stressed that the impressionable young guardians are at all costs to be prevented from imitating the female sex in what are regarded as its characteristic activities—bickering, boasting, uncooperative self-abandonment, blasphemy, and

the frailties of sickness, love and labor. Women, easily deceived by worthless guardians, superstitious, prone to excessive grief, lacking in knowledge of what is good for them, and inferior in intellect and in general to men, are no more fit to serve as role models for the chosen youth [of Athens] than are madmen, craftsmen, or slaves.[4]

In the *Politics,* Aristotle distinguished among those human beings said to be free, those said to be slavish by nature, and those said to be good. Free persons were those capable of orienting themselves and aligning their actions to conform with the common good, not only that of their households, but that of the *polis* or city-state (*Metaphysics,* 12.10, 3).[5] Aristotle contended that slaves lacked the innate or natural disposition toward freedom or virtuous control of their own lives. Consequently, slaves had no share in the responsibility for the household, no share in the city-state, no share in the common good. The free man, the *polites* or citizen, was the one who had the capacity for active participation in political life and in the common good. But, the citizen was never simply identical with any person who resided in or had been born in the geographic boundaries of the *polis:* women, children, slaves, foreigners, metics all inhabited the *polis* without participating in it as citizens. The citizen in the strict sense was "a man who share[d] in the administration of justice and the holding of office" (*Politics,*

1274b, 32). The *polis* was constituted by free *men* of good birth, of potentially good nature, of virtue, of wealth.

While neither Saint Augustine nor Saint Thomas Aquinas contested the social and class structures under which they lived, both these Christian thinkers taught that each human person—male and female, ruler and ruled, lord and serf—was to live a life of virtue in accord with his or her station. Augustine and Aquinas wrote of human freedom primarily, although not exclusively, in relation to God-given free will, human choice, the practice of virtuous habits, and the human response to and reception of divine grace. They understood freedom as integral to human nature; however, freedom was also a gift from God. Freedom was to be exercised in conformity with the will of God, for it is through a lived life of virtue and goodness that human beings have and express their true and only freedom.

Yet, for Augustine women remained a "special symbol of evil."[6] Aquinas argued that regarding individual nature, women are "defective and misbegotten." Although he maintained that women had souls, he reasoned that they did not fully bear the imprint of the *imago Dei* or image of God—this was possible only for men.[7]

The modern philosophers, men like Niccolo Machiavelli, Thomas Hobbes, and John Locke, can be said to present a thoroughgoing rejection of the classical philosophic and theological tradition, except where women were concerned. In Machiavelli, Aristotle's virtuous median gave way to the most base common denominator, thus shifting the ground of virtue:

no longer was it necessary to *be* good, only *to seem to be* good.[8] Virtue was no longer to be reinterpreted in light of how human beings ought to live, but in light of how human beings *actually do live.*

These new political philosophers argued that the individual human being by nature is complete, independent, prior to and above society. The moral fact of civil society was no longer to be understood in terms of duty, but in terms of rights—self-interested, self-regarding passions. These new political philosophers conceived of society as contractual, as an aggregate of autonomous individuals or units cooperating only when the terms of that cooperation advanced the ends or advantage of the parties involved.

The whole of Thomas Hobbes' political philosophy is founded on the argument that the human is to be conceived in terms of the *prehuman* or the *state of nature.* For Hobbes, nature has made all human beings—male and female—equal in faculties of body and mind, but what substantiates that equality is that each one is equally able to kill the others.[9] Men and women live in "continual fear, and danger of violent death; and the life of man is solitary, poor, nasty, brutish, and short."[10] Still, and paradoxically, Hobbes subordinated women to men. The family is a decidedly patriarchal institution: it consists of "a man and his children; or of a man and his servants; or of a man, and his children, and servants together: wherein the Father or Master is sovereign."[11] And in the *Dialogue on the Common Law,* Hobbes declares, "The Father of the Family by the Law of Nature [is] absolute Lord of his Wife and Children."[12] Although women may be equal to men at times, Hobbes understands the patriarchal family as an essentially natural institution.

John Locke appealed to "parental equality to combat absolutism in the political realm," but he argues as well for the subordination of women to men. Where "the things of their common Interest and Property" are concerned, Locke argues, should husband and wife disagree, "the Rule...naturally falls to the Man's share, as the abler and the stronger."[13] For Locke, the natural liberty or freedom of human beings consisted in being free from any superior power, being free from any subjugation to the will or the legislative authority of any other human being. This natural liberty or freedom from absolute or arbitrary power was *necessary* and linked to the instinct for self-preservation; it cannot be relinquished except by consent.[14]

In the New Testament or Christian scriptures, notions and experience of freedom, emancipation, and deliverance are centered on Jesus of Nazareth, the Christ of God. Jesus stands as a sign signifying contradiction: he emptied *(kenosis)* himself of all divinity so as not to outshine authentic human freedom or liberation, yet embraced bondage and servitude. He healed and emancipated broken bodies and spirits, yet went without complaint to an ignominious death on the cross. He delivered us from sin and death, yet suffered and died. "For freedom," the Apostle writes, "Christ has set us free" (Gal 5:1).

Still, where the notions of freedom, emancipation, and deliverance are concerned, the gospels and epistles present more than a few difficulties. Here are three of these: *First,* slavery, the very opposite of freedom, of emancipation, was employed questionably as a spiritual and theological metaphor to provide "a model of dependence and self-surrender."[15] *Second,* slavery in the ancient world was a real condition of social death.[16] Even as the New Testament writers denoted sin metaphorically as slavery, they did not much challenge the cruelty or the existence of slavery. *Third,* slavery provokes the desire for social freedom, but when slavery is so spiritualized that desire is subverted, it gives way to damaging detachment and indifference.

This cursory review of religious and philosophical thinking serves to evoke the contentious and troublesome backgrounds, different, even antagonistic meanings of notions that we hold dear—freedom, emancipation, and deliverance. However, all this surely seems a long way from theology, particularly a theology of freedom rooted in the saving death of Jesus of Nazareth, the Christ of God, and drawn from womanist (and feminist) perspectives. But, the modern (or postmodern) world has been shaped and defined by concrete religious, cultural, and social manifestations of the various meanings of freedom, emancipation, and deliverance. The United States of America is an ambiguous instance of this modern (postmodern) world; these notions shape the matrix of our religious, cultural, and social living. To begin to interrogate freedom, emancipation, and deliverance is to begin to interrogate the social order—that "inclusive horizon" in which we human beings comport ourselves as historical beings.[17] It is from within this modern (postmodern) world that womanist (and feminist) theologies emerge.

II

Liberation theology appeared in the latter half of the 1960s, and, as Theo Witvliet reminds us, its first contours could be seen at roughly the same time in various parts of the world. The vibrant hopes and expectations that liberation theology, or more properly, liberation theologies, carried are related to concrete social (i.e., political, economic, and technological) struggles for justice, for self-determination, for control of national or regional economic and technological resources, and for human equality. The prophetic range and controversial character of these struggles are incarnated in men and women like Mahatma Gandhi, Bernadette Devlin, Betty Friedan, Fannie Lou Hamer, Rosa Parks, and Martin Luther King, Jr.

Liberation theologies broke with oppressive forms of theology, but not with the Christian tradition as such. Rather, these theologies grappled with what the "Christian tradition has handed down in connection with liberation and the relationship between the eschatological reality of God and the historical struggle of human beings, their suffering and their revolt against the powers that oppress them."[18] These theologies pushed for cultural, social, intellectual freedom.

M. Shawn Copeland

The first generation of feminist theology was directed by concerns and assumptions emanating from the secular white women's movement and paralleling those of the theologies of liberation from Latin America, Asia, the United States, and Africa. Feminist theology aimed to uncover the ways in which the Christian tradition had been debased by the ideology of patriarchy—that "male pyramid of graded subordinations and exploitations [that specify women's oppressions in terms of the class, race, country, or religion of the men to whom [the women] 'belong.'"[19] Feminist theology explicitly drew on the experience of women as a source for theological reflection and analysis, thus placing women at the *hermeneutical center* of theology. Through a hermeneutics of suspicion, feminist theology aims to liberate women from repressive societal and ecclesial structures and to uproot those patriarchal ideologies that deny the intrinsic and full personhood of women and deface the divine image in them.

By the late 1970s, white feminists and male liberationists of all races and cultures had adhered to the advice of the great Protestant theologian Karl Barth and taken the gospel in one hand and the newspaper in the other to begin clearing the theological landscape. They exposed the biological, social, cultural, and religious cover stories that had shaped not only our living arrangements but our self-understanding, our self-esteem, and our actions. Yet, neither group sufficiently recognized or interrogated the meaning and significance of the presence of women of color in their midst, and white feminists erred as well by disregarding the intraracial situation of class difference. This neglect threatened the power and the future both of feminist and liberation theologies.

As early as 1970, some black women had begun to expose and contest the "double" and triple jeopardy of our position. Frances Beale, in a very early essay entitled "Double Jeopardy: To Be Black and Female," analyzed the psychological and social exploitation of black women by the dominant white supremacist patriarchal capitalist order.[20] She also set out to correct the myth that feminism was a white woman's issue.

Beale advocated a women's liberation that would sniff out and reject any form of white supremacist and imperialist ideology and that was committed to work concretely for structural societal change. Beale argued that

> any white [women's] group that does not have an anti-imperialist and anti-racist [creed] has absolutely nothing in common with the black women's struggle....If [white women] do not realize that the reasons for their condition lie in the system and not simply that men get a vicarious pleasure out of "consuming their bodies for exploitative reasons," then we cannot unite with them around common grievances.[21]

Neither did Beale spare the black community:

> The black community and black women especially must begin raising questions about the kind of

society we wish to see established....The new world that we are attempting to create must destroy oppression of any type. The value of this new system will be determined by the status of the person who [is lowest]...on the totem pole.[22]

Moreover, she asserted:

To assign women the role of housekeeper and mother while men go forth into battle is a highly questionable doctrine for a revolutionary to maintain....Those who consider themselves to be revolutionary must begin to deal with other revolutionaries as equals. And so far as I know, revolutionaries are not determined by sex.[23]

Beale's voice in this essay is the rhetoric of the '60s; its sound may be dated, but its sentiment, direction, and purpose found a place at October 1997's "Million Women's March."

Womanist theology is the response of black women moral and social ethicists, theologians, philosophers, and cultural critics to the marginalization and suppression of black women's questions and discoveries, theological and pastoral work within the churches, within academic religious discourse, within black theology, and to some extent, within African American culture. For nearly fifteen years, Delores Williams, Katie Cannon, Jacquelyn Grant, Toinette Eugene, and Cheryl Townsend Gilkes have charted a collective course, taking their bearings for moral and theological reflection by the compass of black women's religious, cultural, and social experiences.[24] They christened this enterprise *womanist theology* to honor Alice Walker's creative retrieval and advancement of the rich African American cultural epithet, *womanish.*[25] Walker's definition of womanist is only secondarily religious, it is *primarily* spiritual. It acknowledges, affirms, and testifies to the centrality of the Spirit as the "operative manifestation of God in everyday [African American] life."[26] Womanist theology denotes reflection on religion and religious experience emerging from the distinct perspective of black women; it signifies a shared and complementary constellation of beliefs, practices, commitments, and values. Indeed, womanist theology signifies a paradigm shift in Christian theology.

Christian womanist and feminist theologians, black women and white women, share several basic assumptions in their theological work. *First,* sexism is the subjugation of women to men on the basis of biological difference; sexism projects intrinsic male superiority over against intrinsic female inferiority. On the basis of biological accident, sexism coaches culture to define women as closer to "nature" than men. Hence, women are rendered as means and objects to be subordinated, controlled, and manipulated for the ends of culture (men) by culture (men). *Second*, the results of this appeal to biological accident have permeated and distorted the whole of the historical and religious tradition so thoroughly that the inferiority of women and their necessary submission to patriarchy in church and in society have come to be understood as natural and divinely ordained. *Third,* womanist and feminist theologies aim to free women from repressive societal and ecclesial structures and to uproot those ideologies that deny the intrinsic personhood of women and deface the divine image in them. *Fourth,* womanist and feminist theologies refer explicitly to the experience of women as a proper source for theological reflection and analysis. Women stand at the hermeneutical center of womanist and feminist theologies. *Fifth,* womanist and feminist theologies expose and oppose concrete cultural, social (i.e., political, economic, technological), ethnic, and racial divisions among women, as well as the sources and traditions of those divisions. *Sixth,* womanists and many feminists insist that these theologies cannot reduplicate the sin of gender oppression. Women cannot simply scapegoat males for historical evil in a way that renders them innocent and passive victims; nor can women affirm themselves as bearing the fullness of the imprint of the *imago Dei,* subjects of full human potential in a way that diminishes male humanity. And, *seventh,* many feminists and some womanists have begun to turn attention to created life beyond that of human life, to repair the way in which we have diminished God's "other beings in the community of creation."[27]

Despite such fundamental agreement, womanists frequently and boisterously disagree with (white) feminists. Womanists are angered by the ways in which (white) feminist theologians, with casual entitlement, appropriate African

American culture (e.g., jazz or aesthetics or literature) while ignoring the concrete struggle against racism and its vicious effects. Womanists are dismayed by the rhetoric of solidarity that white feminists routinely employ but are slow to practice. Womanists are discouraged by the reticence of white feminists to explore critically the meaning and practice of "whiteness" in identity politics. At the same time, however, there are differences among womanists about issues of theological method, content, and practice. These are important, but relatively minor in comparison to some crucial differences among some womanists in thinking about the relation of Jesus of Nazareth and his cross to the freedom, emancipation, and deliverance of women.

III

The teaching, preaching, and practices of Jesus of Nazareth were directed toward freedom, emancipation, and deliverance. Through his other-directed ministry, his humble death, he freed women and men—all humanity—from the bonds of physical and cosmic evil, from personal and structural sin, from death.

The journey of mercy and service that earned him death on a cross began in a small synagogue in his hometown. Filled with the Spirit, this native son takes the scroll from the attendant. Those assembled expect some words of substance, nothing novel or too innovative, but solid, perhaps, even thoughtful commentary:

M. Shawn Copeland

The Spirit of the Lord is upon me, because he has anointed me to preach good news to the poor. He has sent me to proclaim release to the captives and recovering of sight to the blind, to set at liberty those who are oppressed, to proclaim the acceptable year of the Lord. (Luke 4:18–19)

Luke's narrative strategically places the prophecy of Isaiah at the beginning of Jesus' ministry, hence prophecy functions programmatically. Jesus makes these words his own. Jesus understands himself to be sent to those whom the ancient world considered irrevocably afflicted and enduring divine punishment for sin: those children, women, and men who could not hear, who could not speak, who could not see; those who were paralyzed or crippled, who were impoverished. The mission of Jesus is to those who are outcast, brokenhearted, imprisoned, downtrodden, ritually unclean, and oppressed; to those who are without choice, without hope, and without a future. To these children, women, and men, Jesus proclaims freedom, emancipation, and deliverance. To these children, women, and men, Jesus announces the reign, the kingdom of God and pledges that that kingdom is for them.

Jesus' ministry is marked by the exorcising of demons, the healing of lepers, the raising from the dead of an only son and an only daughter of distraught parents, the healing of men and women with fevers, diseases, and various physical deformities. Jesus eats and drinks with women and men of questionable character—tax collectors, outcasts, prostitutes, and known sinners. When questioned about his associates, he replies, "Those who are well have no need of a physician, but those who are sick; I have not come to call the righteous, but sinners to repentance" (Luke 5:31–32).

The God whom Jesus knows and loves, whom he encourages his disciples to address in prayer as Father (Luke 11:1–4) is a God "of tenderness and compassion, slow to anger, and rich in mercy" (Jonah 4:2). Jesus knows and loves this God as the One who hears and responds in steadfast love to the cry of the little ones who suffer from afflictions of every sort, and who have no other home but the kingdom of God. Jesus loves this God with a single-mindedness of heart that compels him to a ministry of compassion and that allows him to subordinate observance of the Sabbath to legitimate human need.

Luke's Gospel is punctuated by the active presence of women. The young Mary who gave birth to Jesus is no passive victim in his conception: she is asked, not forced; her integrity is respected. At the ritual of purification following childbirth, the prophet Anna recognizes the child: "[She] gave thanks to God, and spoke of him to all who were looking for the redemption of Jerusalem" (Luke 2:36–39). Women are among those who are cured, exorcised, healed, and forgiven; their experiences provide content for Jesus' parables. But, more important, women are a part of the group of disciples who travels with Jesus to various cities and villages; women participate in the ministry of Jesus. Luke names them: Mary Magdalene; Joanna, the wife of

Herod's steward; Susanna; Mary, the mother of James; and many others (Luke 8:1–3). When the woman named Mary chooses to sit at the feet of Jesus as a disciple, he sides with her in that choice over against the role set for women by Jewish culture, society, and religion (Luke 10:38–42). And, finally, the very proclamation of the resurrection itself is entrusted to women; their remembrance of the very words of Jesus (and they could not remember what they themselves had not heard) grounds their witness (Luke 24:9).

In reaching out to those who experience exclusion and ostracism, in forgiving and admonishing sinners, in curing fevers and disease and deformity, in driving out demons, in submitting minute interpretation of the Law to compassion, Jesus struggled to create a context for the coming reign of God. He gathered together into a unified group those who responded to his proclamation of the reign of God without preference to gender, social class, personal background, and previous history. Characteristic of this group of women and men was the sharing of a common meal in celebration of this new relationship with God and with one another, which they enjoyed on the basis of their response to the proclamation of the reign of God. He enacts and actuates the meanings of freedom, emancipation, and deliverance.

Although this sketch is quite telescopic, it does familiarize us with the basic concerns of Jesus' ministry and grounds the following observations:

1. Jesus associates himself with those whose pain and needs are given voice by the prophet Isaiah: the poor, the captives, the blind, the oppressed are those women and men who primarily claim Jesus' attention and compassionate concern. Indeed, Jesus displays a decisive concern for them.

2. The proclamation of the reign of God is at the heart of Jesus' preaching. While the reign of God is never to be identified with any particular concrete historical phenomenon, it has its roots in present existential reality. It is in our midst (Luke 17:21). To speak of the reign of God is to speak of the divine exercise of power on behalf of those who hear the call of God and who respond in prayer, in penance, in *metanoia*, that is, in conversion of mind, of heart, of life, thus creating a living and lived context for the coming reign of God.

3. Jesus gathered disciples around him, and they participated in his healing power, which was a sign for Jesus that the kingdom of God was breaking through.

4. Jesus' preaching rejects all those values and practices that run counter to his own growing vision of life lived under God's reign.

5. The resurrection is the ratifying source and foundation of the faith of those women and men who asserted on the day of Pentecost that "God had

made [this Jesus who had been crucified] both Lord and Christ" (Acts 2:36). The earliest followers of the "way" that Jesus taught came to understand the resurrection as God's vindication of Jesus' life example and mission, as God's mighty exercise of judgment, love, and deliverance on behalf of the cause and person of Jesus of Nazareth.

IV

The narratives of the cross of Jesus and the reception of those narratives have never been, nor can they ever be, personally, theologically, or socially neutral. In a letter to a group of the earliest followers of "the way" at Corinth, Paul called the cross "a stumbling block" and a "folly."[28] This assessment remains true, in certain ways, of the cross today. In *Sisters in the Wilderness,* womanist theologian Delores Williams launches a critical dialogue with the cross and the doctrine of redemption in relation to the experience of black women.[29] On the one hand, the doctrine of the redemption represents Jesus as "the ultimate surrogate figure….Surrogacy, attached to this divine personage, thus takes on an aura of the sacred."[30] On the other hand, black women's lives have been shaped by "social-role surrogacy." Williams takes her cues from the biblical experience of Hagar, who served as a surrogate womb for Abraham's seed and from the ambiguous possibilities opened by current reproductive technologies, which putatively have liberated middle- and upper-class white women from the time and labor of childbearing.[31] Historically, black women have been (mis)used or coerced to take on roles that ordinarily would have been fulfilled by someone else, including that of surrogate mother or caretaker. Williams asks, "Will poverty pressure poor black women to rent their bodies out as incubators for wealthier women unable to birth children?"[32]

Williams asserts that the "place of the cross in any theology significantly informed by African-American women's experience of surrogacy 'faces' a major theological problem." With her characteristic bluntness and intellectual daring, she writes:

> Even if one buys into the notion of the cross as the meeting place of the will of God to give up the Son (coerced surrogacy?) and the will of the Son to give up himself (voluntary surrogacy?) so that "the spirit of abandonment and self-giving love" proceeds from the cross "to raise up abandoned men," African-American women are still left with the questions: Can there be salvific power for black women in Christian images of oppression (for example Jesus on the cross) meant to teach something about redemption?[33]

Williams draws out the profound challenge to Christian theology, and especially to any theology that comes from those who are most marginalized in a society—particularly, poor, despised women (and men) of color. It is these women (and men) who are condemned by the powerful and privileged as both the guilty who deserve suffering and the suffering servants called to imitate the crucified Jesus.

Here, before the cross, Williams takes up the task of biblical hermeneutics. She reasons that in such a racist and patriarchal situation, womanists, indeed all women, must demythologize their readings, sweep ever so rigorously against the grain.[34] After critical and careful biblical exegesis and research, Williams offers two conclusions: First, she reminds us that although black male liberation theologians have used androcentric biblical paradigms to support their theological statements, the wider black community has used the Bible quite differently. For more than a century, the community has "appropriated the Bible in such a way that black women's experience figured just as eminently as black men's in the community's memory, in its self-understanding and in its understanding of God's relation to its life."[35] And second, Williams cautions us that, although the enslaved people claim the Exodus story as their own and situate Jesus' interpretation of the prophecy of Isaiah in Luke 4 at the center of theological statements about freedom and emancipation, womanist theologians must reckon with the historicity of that claim and its centrality. To do otherwise, Williams asserts, is to "ignore generations of black history subsequent to slavery...to consign the community and the black theological imagination to a kind of historical stalemate that denies the possibility of change with regard to the people's experience of God and with regard to the possibility of God changing in relation to the community."[36]

Given the very historicity of our situation, we are confronted by a new cultural and theological situation: "the black experience...as a female-and-male inclusive wilderness experience."[37] The bitter realities of poverty, exploitation, marginalization, and violence along with hopelessness, alienation, nihilism, and despair confirm this proposal. Given black women's historic experience of sexism in all Christian churches, Williams drives home the anxiety, difficulty, pain, and confusion that black women might well experience as they stand near the cross of Jesus. Indeed, black women (and men) have made Jesus' cry of abandonment our own: "My God, my God, why have you forsaken me?"[38]

The work of womanist Jacquelyn Grant presents a different discussion of black women's apprehension of Jesus of Nazareth.[39] *In White Women's Christ, Black Women's Jesus: Feminist Christology and Womanist Response,* while Grant concentrates on establishing the differences between (white, liberal) feminist and womanist theological positions, she clearly sets out her starting point as black women's faith and the importance of the biblical witness. Grant's account accents the humanity (rather than gender) of Jesus and his ministry on behalf of the oppressed: his proclamation of the coming reign of God; his lived life of mutuality, interdependence, and regard; his healing and mercy; his self-sacrifice for our deliverance. There is no artificial separation between the person of Jesus and his work. Moreover, the designation of Jesus as *messiah* or *Christ* is due not to his maleness, but to his incarnate and selfless *(kenotic)* identification with the poor.

Grant's text exposes the "imprisonment" of Jesus Christ by patriarchy, white supremacy, and class privilege. Moreover, that text works for his liberation or redemption, his freedom and deliverance in the experiences of black women. In the essay, "Subjectification as a Requirement for Christological Construction," Grant examines the question Jesus put to his disciples: "Who do you say that I am?" (Mark 8:29). Grant argues that with this question Jesus calls his disciples, indeed all believers, women and men of all ages, to a newfound human subjectivity predicated on their commitment to struggle against all that dehumanizes and oppresses.[40] With this question, the disciples are summoned to examine just who Jesus is for them and the meaning of his ministry. With his questioning, Jesus recognizes the disciples as *subjects,* that is, experiencing, inquiring, judging, reflecting, deciding, acting, responsible human persons who are centers of value in love. Moreover, Jesus offers subjectivity to women and men who are among the most marginalized and oppressed groups in his society.

Although we might consider subjectification an awkward or clumsy term, it does clarify the aim of Grant's analysis. Subjectification refers *first* to the invitation offered to all, the invitation to make a decision for Jesus—who he is, what his message and ministry mean. *Second,* the term opposes the commodification of humanity, particularly the commodification of women (and men) of African descent, and the objectification of women as sexual merchandise. *Third,* subjectification implies active taking on, assuming, affirming of one's own personhood, one's own humanity, one's own subjectivity. Moreover, if black women are to be subjects, to claim and act out of their own personhood, their own humanity, they must engage in three battles: the battle against the ever-pervasive racism of the dominant culture; the battle against sexism of the dominant male culture; and the battle against the sexism of black men. Black women struggle in the name of Jesus to effect the realization of their essential human freedom. They are inspired by his active hope in resurrected, liberated existence.

V

What might it mean to offer the cross as a model to poor, despised black women? What might it mean to offer the cross as a example to abused and violated women? What might it mean to tell young black or Latino women and men who are belittled or physically assaulted each day that God in Jesus is also alienated, a stranger, a despised "other"? Can memory of the passion and death of Jesus uncover our pretense to personal and communal innocence, to social and religious neutrality before structural evil and suffering? Can the cross of Jesus give concrete form and meaning to the emancipation, liberation, and deliverance of oppressed children, women, and men around the globe? What transpires in the gaze between black women and the crucified Jesus? What kind of theology of the cross can meet the example of Jesus of Nazareth, his freedom and consciousness of God, his aims and solidarity? What kind of theology of the cross is needed in our situation? In conclusion, I propose three theses toward a theology of freedom that is grounded in the mystery of the cross.

1. *Jesus of Nazareth is the clearest example of what it means to identify with the oppressed, to take their side in the struggle for life—no matter the cost.* He is *freedom incarnate.* To be freedom incarnate, to incarnate freedom is to realize in a life lived in response to the grace of God. To take up the theology of the cross is to repudiate any form of masochism, even Christian masochism. Even if we insist that the cross is the mysterious meeting place of divine grace and human freedom, that the cross is the priceless measure of self-transcending love, that the cross of Jesus is the transcendent solution to the problem of evil—a theology of the cross is obliged to question suffering. By acknowledging with full seriousness the vicious and political character of crucifixion in the ancient world, a renewed theology of the cross must renounce any tendency to encourage suffering as preferable or acceptable.

2. *The cross signifies God's own struggle against the powers and principalities of this world.* The cross manifests God's desire to emancipate those who are in psychic, cultural, or social bondage. Only through a praxis of struggle *beside* and *on behalf of* the marginalized in our society can we grasp the meaning of freedom, of liberation. At the same

time, freedom is risky business: the deep, demanding desire for freedom, for liberation, for emancipation is not, in and of itself, or in fact, freedom, liberation, emancipation. Moreover, if that desire is substituted for liberation, it can become a dangerous illusion that can only aid the powers of oppression. Freedom is risky business: it is so much more about duty, obligation, and regard than it is about license and rights.

To take up a theology of the cross for a new millennium is to grasp not only the crucified Jesus "in the light and context of his resurrection and, therefore, of freedom and hope,"[41] but the ineluctable relation between the poor, oppressed, and marginalized and the constitution and self-realization of the community of the Resurrected Lord. Any renewed theology of the cross must be dissatisfied with any notion of salvation that either surrenders the social and structural to the individual and personal or evades the holistic demands of the authentic struggle of lived Christian life. Thus a renewed theology of the cross illumines the social function of religion and situates any legal or distributive or retributive demands of justice in the context of a solidarity that cherishes a self-transcending love committed to undo and repair injustice.

3. *The real meaning of the cross of Jesus is a mystery of freedom enacted for our deliverance.* We must not forget that crucifixion, primarily, was a military and political punishment, the supreme Roman penalty. It was used against

political insurrectionists, rebellious slaves, murderers, and robbers. In nearly all instances, crucifixion was reserved for men and women of the lower classes, slaves, and subjugated peoples. Crucifixion was intended to intimidate by example and subdue by display; it was high state theatrical violence. We can begin to imagine the shock experienced by the disciples and the crowd gathered around Jesus when he said, "If any want to become my followers, let them deny themselves and take up their cross and follow me" (Mark 8:34). Such a message would scarcely have been attractive. The ordinary people of the ancient world were well aware of what it meant to be flogged, to bear the cross through the city, and then to be nailed to it. Surely, they feared crucifixion and wanted no part of it.

But the word of the cross is life, and those who heed that word are saved. For them the cross is the power of God; but for those who cannot embrace its mystery, the cross is a folly, a stumbling block. For the apostle Paul, the cross projects a distinctive horizon or worldview. Those who heed the word of the cross enter into a new reality, a new interpretative order grounded on new values and meanings, resulting in new choices and actions.

The power of God in the cross represents a logic radically different than human logic. Human logic is a logic of equivalence, a forensic logic—the punishment must fit the crime; justice means fairness. Human logic is patient of order and design. Divine logic, God's logic, is a logic of "excess, of superabundance."[42] The power of God in the cross is its paradox—the resurrection, unexpected, unimagined. Divine logic is interruptive: it reveals and projects the hidden merciful love of God into the most bleak of circumstances. Divine logic releases us: it frees us from the gravity that impedes the human spirit, that anesthetizes our deepest desires for more fruitful, more creative living and loving. Divine logic nudges us to risk: to risk disease and discomfort with whatever obscures the sight of the glory of God on another's face; to risk the consequences of struggle for just reconciliation in the thick of glaring division.

Notes

1. *The Passover Haggadah,* ed. Nahum Glazer (New York: Schocken Books, 1969), 49; see Michael Walzer, *Exodus and Revolution* (New York: Basic Books, 1985). While legislation for Passover appears to be given at Sinai, the actual prescriptions for the celebration are established c. 600 B.C.E.
2. David Brion Davis, *The Problem of Slavery in Western Culture* (Ithaca, NY: Cornell University Press, 1966), 67.
3. Susan Moller Okin, *Women in Western Political Thought* (Princeton, NJ: Princeton University Press, 1979), 22.
4. Ibid., 23.
5. Aristotle, *Metaphysics,* trans. Hugh Tredennick (1935; 1936; 1947; 1958; Cambridge, MA: Harvard University, Loeb, 1962); citations from the *Metaphysics* are followed in the text in brackets.
6. Margaret A. Farley, "Sources of Sexual Inequality in the History of Christian Thought," *Journal of Religion* 56, no. 2 (April 1976): 37.
7. Thomas Aquinas, *Summa Theologiae,* trans. Blackfriars (New York: McGraw-Hill, 1966), Pars Prima, 90–93.

M. Shawn Copeland

8. Niccolo Machiavelli, *The Prince* [1513], trans. ed. Mark Musa (New York: St. Martin's Press, 1964), xviii.
9. Thomas Hobbes, *Leviathan* (1651), ed. C. B. Macpherson, *Leviathan* (1968; Harmondsworth: Penguin Books Ltd., 1981, 1982, 1983), I, xi.
10. Ibid., I, xiii.
11. Ibid., xx; Okin, *Women in Western Political Thought,* 198–99.
12. Hobbes, *A Dialogue Between a Philosopher and a Student of the Common Laws of England,* ed. Joseph Cropsey (Chicago: University of Chicago Press, 1971), 139, cited in Okin, *Women in Western Political Thought,* 198.
13. John Locke, *An Essay Concerning the True Original Extent and End of Civil Government* ed. Ernest Barker (1960; London: Oxford, 1980), II, 57–59, 63; II, 82–83.
14. Ibid., II, 22–23.
15. Davis, *Problem of Slavery in Western Culture,* 90.
16. See Orlando Patterson, *Slavery and Social Death: A Comparative Study* (Cambridge, MA: Harvard University Press, 1982), idem, *Freedom in the Making of Western Culture* (New York: Basic Books, 1991).
17. Jürgen Moltmann, "Toward a Political Hermeneutics of the Gospel," *New Theology,* No. 6, ed. Martin Marty and Dean G. Peerman (New York: Macmillan Company, 1969), 81; Glenn Tinder, *The Crisis of Political Imagination* (New York: Charles Scribner's Sons, 1964), 298.
18. Ibid., xviii.
19. Elisabeth Schüssler Fiorenza, *Bread, Not Stone: The Challenge of Feminist Biblical Interpretation* (1984; Boston: Beacon Press, 1995), xiv.
20. Frances Beale, "Double Jeopardy: To Be Black and Female," 90–100, in *The Black Woman: An Anthology,* ed. Toni Cade (New York: A Mentor Book/North American Library, 1970).
21. Ibid., 98–99.
22. Ibid.

23. Ibid.
24. See Delores S. Williams, "Women's Oppression and Lifeline Politics in Black Women's Religious Narratives," *Journal of Feminist Studies in Religion* 2 (Fall 1985): 59–71; idem, "The Color of Feminism: Or Speaking the Black Woman's Tongue," *Journal of Religious Thought* 43 (Spring/Summer 1986): 42–58; Katie Geneva Cannon, *Black Womanist Ethics* (Atlanta, GA: Scholars Press, 1988); idem, "Hitting a Straight Lick with a Crooked Stick: The Womanist Dilemma in the Development of a Black Liberation Ethic," *The Annual: The Society of Christian Ethics* (1987): 165–77.

 Jacquelyn Grant was not the first to raise the issue of sexism in the black church, but she may be the first to raise this issue in the male-dominated context of black theology in "Black Theology and the Black Woman," 418–33, in Gayraud S. Wilmore and James H. Cone, eds., *Black Theology: A Documentary History, 1966–1979* (New York: Orbis Books, 1979); and Cheryl Townsend Gilkes, "The Role of Women in the Sanctified Church," *Journal of Religious Thought* 43 (Spring/Summer 1986): 24–41; idem, "The Roles of Church and Community Mothers: Ambivalent American Sexism or Fragmented African Familyhood?" *Journal of Feminist Studies in Religion* 2, no. 1 (Spring 1986): 41–59.

25. Alice Walker, *In Search of Our Mothers' Gardens: Womanist Prose by Alice Walker* (New York: Harcourt Brace Jovanovich Publishers, 1983):
 Womanist 1. From womanish. (Opp. of "girlish," i.e., frivolous, irresponsible, not serious.) A black feminist or feminist of color. From the black folk expression of mothers to female children, "You acting womanish," i.e., like a woman. Usually, referring to outrageous, audacious, courageous or *willful* behavior. Wanting to know more and in greater depth than is considered "good" for one. Interested in grown-up doings. Acting grown up. Being grown up. Interchangeable with another black folk

expression: "You trying to be grown." Responsible. In charge. *Serious.*

Also: A woman who loves other women, sexually and/or nonsexually. Appreciates and prefers women's culture, women's emotional flexibility (values tears as natural counterbalance of laughter), and women's strength. Sometimes loves individual men, sexually and/or nonsexually. Committed to survival and wholeness of entire people, male and female. Not a separatist, except periodically for health. Traditionally universalist, as in: "Mama, why are we brown, pink, and yellow, and our cousins are white, beige, and black?" Ans.: "Well, you know the colored race is just like a flower garden, with every color flower represented." Traditionally capable, as in: "Mama, I'm walking to Canada and I'm taking you and a bunch of other slaves with me." Reply: "It wouldn't be the first time."

Loves music. Loves dance. Loves the moon. *Loves* the Spirit. Loves love and food and roundness. Loves struggle. *Loves* the Folk. Loves herself. *Regardless.* (xi)

26. Cheryl Townsend Gilkes, "Roundtable Response," *Journal of Feminist Studies in Religion 5*, no. 2 (Fall 1989): 106.
27. Rosemary Radford Ruether, *Sexism and God-Talk: Toward a Feminist Theology* (1983; Boston: Beacon Press, 1993), 20.
28. Ibid.
29. Delores S. Williams, *Sisters in the Wilderness: The Challenge of Womanist God-Talk* (Maryknoll, NY: Orbis Books, 1993).
30. Ibid., 162.
31. Ibid., 60–61, 82.
32. Ibid., 82; see also Dorothy Roberts, *Killing the Black Body: Race, Reproduction, and the Meaning of Liberty* (New York: Pantheon Books, 1997).
33. Ibid., 162. Williams is quoting Jürgen Moltmann, "The Crucified God: God and the Trinity Today," in *New Questions of God,* ed. Johannes B. Metz (New York: Herder & Herder, 1972), 33–35.

34. Delores S. Williams, "Black Women's Surrogacy Experience and the Christian Notion of Redemption," in *After Patriarchy: Feminist Transformations of the World Religions,* ed., Paula Cooey et al. (Maryknoll, NY: Orbis Books, 1991), 1–14.

35. Williams, *Sisters in the Wilderness,* 1–2.

36. Ibid., 151, 153.

37. Ibid., 149.

38. John S. Pobee, "Bible Study in Africa: A Passover of Language," *Semeia* 73 (1996): 167.

39. Jacquelyn Grant, *White Women's Christ, Black Women's Jesus: Feminist Christology and Womanist Response:* (Atlanta, GA: Scholars Press, 1989); idem, "Womanist Theology: Black Women's Experience as a Source for Doing Theology, with Special Reference to Christology," *Journal of the Interdenominational Theological Center* 13, no. 2 (Spring 1986): 195–212; idem, "The Sin of Servanthood and the Deliverance of Discipleship," in Emilie M. Townes, ed., *A Troubling in My Soul: Womanist Perspectives on Evil and Suffering* (Maryknoll, NY: Orbis Books, 1993), 199–218.

40. Jacquelyn Grant, "Womanist Jesus and the Mutual Struggle for Liberation," in *The Recovery of Black Presence: An Introductory Exploration,* ed. Randall C. Bailey and Jacquelyn Grant (Nashville: Abingdon Press, 1995), 129–42; idem, "Subjectification as a Requirement for Christological Construction," in *Lift Every Voice: Constructing Christian Theologies from the Underside,* ed. Susan Brooks Thistlethwaite and Mary Potter Engel (San Francisco: Harper & Row, Publishers, 1990), 201–14.

41. Jürgen Moltmann, *The Crucified God: The Cross of Christ as the Foundation and Criticism of Christian Theology,* trans. R. A. Wilson and John Bowden (New York: Harper & Row Publishers, 1974), 4.

42. Paul Ricoeur, *Figuring the Sacred: Religion, Narrative, and Imagination* (Minneapolis, MN: Fortress, 1995), 279.

4.

Feminism and the Sacredness of Place

Rosemary Luling Haughton

As a stark beginning to this essay, which is, in essence, very hopeful, I remind you of some grim facts about the global situation:

- Destruction of the ozone layer continues (sheep in southern Chile go blind and the children there have to protect their eyes and skin when they go out of doors).

- Global warming is a reality denied only by a few scientists employed by oil and car companies. The current effects are unpredictable and catastrophic weather systems are already a reality; the future ones are a further melting of the polar ice caps and rise in sea levels; other probable effects include huge shifts in population due to drought and famine for those that can't shift.

- Species (animals, insects, plants) are disappearing every day, including some we haven't even named.

- Child labor is widespread: if they survive, the young workers are dismissed (with no marketable skills) at twenty and are replaced with others half their age.

- Factory workers worldwide are grossly underpaid and work in unsafe conditions. Farm and industrial workers are regularly exposed to toxic chemicals.

- Family farms are destroyed by agribusiness, especially genetically modified crops.

- Forests are cut down and the resulting soil erosion can create new deserts.

- In inner cities worldwide, including in the United States, overcrowded and unsafe slums yield profits for landlords, and governments refuse to dedicate tax money to affordable housing, but happily inflate their "defense" budgets.

Why have all those things happened, and why do they continue to happen? The short answer is that these are the result of treating both people and the Earth herself as *things* to be used, a means to an end, and the end is the enrichment of a few. This is called "commodification." It means thinking of everything—including people—as commodity. Land, the Earth itself, is to be conquered, bought, sold, exploited simply for profit. Even food is thought of not as nourishment but primarily as a source of profit—profit for global corporations. They do their best to control the seed, the chemicals. The agricultural colleges they control tell farmers what they have to use, and corporations control the processes the food undergoes (more chemicals), the huge distributing businesses, and the chains of retailers. And the World Trade Organization is there to make sure no elected government— let alone consumers—can challenge this control. (But, thank God, the protests in Seattle and other places since have done something to change that). Water, too, that most basic essential for all life, is controlled in order to run industries that pollute it and to raise thirsty crops in unsuitable arid conditions, at the expense of those who really need it.

This is a long list—yet only a fraction of what could be said; you can all add to it. And you may be wondering what all this bad news has to do with feminism and sacred place?

To answer this I begin by telling the story of my own discovery of feminism, and of sacred place, and the connection between them and the connection that I see with all that I've just outlined.

I became a Catholic at the age of sixteen, full of enthusiasm and ignorance—and curiosity. I went to conferences and met people who called themselves "Distributists," based on the Catholic social doctrine of *subsidiarity,* which most Catholics have never heard of. It means that you shouldn't control from the center anything that can be efficiently and justly managed at a more local level. (This is something the church has forgotten to apply to its own system of control, unfortunately.) Distributists believe in this distribution of power, and in particular that ownership of land should not be, as in the communist system, owned by the state, but rather locally owned by local people—farmers and small landowners.

Some of the Distributists went beyond theory and set up small communities and bought land themselves to farm on ecologically sound principals, though only scientists had ever heard the word *ecology* at that time—the 1930s and '40s. The Distributists chose a simple, often communal, lifestyle, and were of course derided as unpractical "back-to-the-landers" by those who, even then, saw the future of farming in larger and larger farms and more chemicals. They thought that people who chose to live simply (for spiritual reasons, though it was considered okay to do it for one's health) were nut cases! In hindsight, these eccentrics (and they *were* eccentric!) look less foolish.

At the same time I became involved in Catholic youth movements, and in Paris in 1946 I met young people who actually *read* papal encyclicals about social justice and believed that a new Europe could arise. We proclaimed solidarity with the poor and looked to the church to lead the way toward a just society. We were very young!

It was a few years after I was married that I read a book called *Fertility Farming;* I think it was lent to me by one of those back-to-the-landers. The word *organic* was not then used in that context, but the book was about one farmer's successful efforts to convert his farm to organic methods, using no chemical fertilizers and with crop rotation and natural methods of pest and weed control. He grew more and healthier crops and animals on the same acreage as neighboring farmers, who thought he was laughable until some agreed to see for themselves. In my little back yard I tried to follow these methods, make compost, do companion planting. I was learning to respect the land, respect the extraordinary generativity of the soil. At the same time I was rediscovering the ancient Catholic rituals and their connection to the cycles of the year and the seasons, as my children and I organized our own rituals of blessing the garden and celebrating the harvest.

An old enthusiasm for medieval history re-enforced awareness of the way the celebration of the land was in direct continuity with the older religions, which populated every field, mountain, and stream with deity, celebrating God in the land, and seeing a direct connection between faithfulness to God and the fertility of the soil. It was there in Hebrew scripture, I realized, when famine and drought were seen as the result of unfaithfulness. This connection has been regarded as belonging to "primitive" religion until now, when the connection between human sin and a destroyed land is all too obvious.

About this time in my life, Rachel Carson's book *Silent Spring* first alerted the general public to the probable results of the use of pesticides, and more voices—still few and easily dismissed—began to warn of the consequences of use of toxic chemicals not only in farming but in manufacturing. Thomas Merton in his books wryly commented on the way even monastic farming was getting sucked into the current of "modern" agriculture. He had a sense of the land as sacred, and he was uneasy at the "commodified" attitudes he saw.

So, I began to understand that something horrible was happening to the land, and that this was a desecration, a blasphemy, an offense against God, and this offense was "sin" in the biblical sense—not of personal sinful acts but of people becoming involved in a sinful system and suffering the results, even though they were ignorant of the issues. I tried to teach my own children to understand this. I bought one of them a subscription to the magazine of Britain's Soil Association, the main organization presenting and fostering organic methods of farming and gardening. The children helped to work our garden and, later, we participated as a family in a therapeutic community venture that helped mentally ill people by involving them in the daily life of a farm and large garden (and also in building a huge house to replace the trailers we had been living in). When the children grew up, one (the one who got the subscription) developed a business selling all kinds of organic foods through a direct delivery service. (His dream had been to be a farmer, but he could not find the capital in a hugely expensive market for this "commodity" of land.) Another opened a very successful restaurant serving organic food, became involved in teaching children in local schools how to cook it and in promoting awards for organic food producers and retailers. Others worked with environmental organizations like Friends of the Earth. And they knew the issues as spiritual issues—that is what drives them.

What about feminism? What has that to do with the slowly growing awareness of the violated sacredness of the land, the place where people and crops grow? It took me a while. Even when I began to earn a living as a writer, I did it at home. So I never had to compete in the job market and had no personal experience of discrimination or harassment. Like most women, for a long time I just accepted the usual attitudes toward women. But I remember the day when it dawned on me that when my mother had told me, "There have been no great women artists," she had never asked herself why. She—and I following her—had never wondered how women could have developed any artistic talent they might have when they had no chance to study, were confined either to home or menial work, and in any case were brought up believing that women's talents could be no more than trivial adornments. Asking myself that question was a turning point for me, and of course I later discovered some of the women artists who did indeed produce great work, often because their fathers encouraged them.

I mention this to remind us that this awareness of what had been done to women, which is now commonplace, was slow to grow, and not just for me. We just didn't see it. We deplored stories of open cruelty, but we didn't see the pattern of myth that made cruelty possible and even acceptable. Another bit of education for me happened when a woman who lived across the street from our family left her husband

and revealed that she had been routinely abused, sexually and in other ways, for years. Nobody knew. She said, "I thought maybe marriage was like that," and she had felt there was something wrong with *her*. A local priest had tried to persuade her to go back to her husband, and, locally, the *husband* was the one who got most of the sympathy.

But in the end it was my work as a theologian over many years that made all the connections clear. It happened because I began to develop and share what I called a "theology of exchange," which grew from the work being done in biology and physics, demonstrating the profound interdependence of all reality, so that God could not be perceived as separate but as pouring out life as creation, giving and receiving in a passionate exchange of love and life. I realized that the apparently strange and mysterious doctrine of the Trinity was really an expression of the fact that ultimate reality—God—is not monolithic but is an eternal giving and receiving of being. I began to understand that sin, in essence, meant the attempt to contradict or interrupt the exchange of life, an exchange that is the nature of reality. Anything that exploits, destroys, or abuses, that deceives and distorts and denies that reality, is an offense against the nature of God. I began to see that what happened to women and land were linked: both were regarded as commodities, things to be used for others' purposes.

In the past twenty years of living and working at Wellspring House, I have shared life with women in the family shelter that is part of our work, and in our education programs that help women move out of poverty. The stories of abuse—physical and sexual violence, but also routine denigration of women by partners, fathers, judges, police, media—are my daily experience. I was a feminist before I went there, but that experience has radicalized me. I see the political attitudes that keep women poor and justify abuse, and I see the connection with the exploitation and abuse of land, plants, and animals. I came to see abuse of the land as a feminist issue. The same "commodity" view embraces women and land: land, like women, is seen as something to be used, exploited for the profit of the people with power.

I have a friend, Edwina Gately, who founded (among other things) Genesis House in Chicago as a place for prostitutes hoping to find a new direction. She wrote to me recently about taking some of the women for a few days' retreat at a farm community. They learned to spin wool, collected eggs, helped with farm chores, had an experience of the interaction of people and land. It was transformative for them, opening up depths of feeling they didn't understand. These women had been turned into commodities and had gotten used to that and had a hard time imagining or accepting relationships that were not exploitative. On that farm they saw people living with each other and with the land, in partnership. Abuse of the land *is* a feminist issue.

This brings me back to the history of feminism, which has been written primarily as the story of the struggle for women's civil rights. There are many women now who don't realize that until fewer than 150 years ago women had no right to their own earnings, or to their children if couples separated. Huge advances have been made, though we still have a long way to go. As women then saw it, the struggle for women's rights, especially the vote, was a struggle to make the world a better place for women, for family—for people.

Early feminists were Victorians, brought up to see the home as a sacred place for which they were responsible. Woman's job, they had been taught, was to make the home a place of peace and morality, apart from the wicked world. The women who fought for the vote didn't all think of themselves as feminists; some were fighting against things that could destroy the home. Women got the vote first of all in Wyoming because they persuaded the legislation that women's votes were needed to tame the wild frontier mentality and create an orderly "home" for Wyoming people; to quite an extent they succeeded. Women organized to fight against slavery, against tenement housing, against liquor, against child labor, and to promote clean water and food, public sewage, libraries, parks and recreation, education and training for girls, public transportation, and peace. They saw all these things as extending the sacred sphere of the home to the wider society. All this was part of a morally motivated movement of women that gradually became politicized because more and more women saw that without the vote and the right to public office, without professional opportunities for women as doctors, lawyers, and legislators, none of their goals could be reached. It was a long fight for equality and it's not over; but it was, as Susan B. Anthony said, "not for ourselves alone." It was for justice for all.

These suffragists were mostly middle class, and many working-class women didn't care much about the vote—their concerns were more immediate. At about the same time, though separately, working women were organizing for decent wages and working conditions, and for the right to unionize. The working men had created the unions in order to work—and if necessary strike—for better conditions, hours, and wages, but the women had to fight the unions too. Men's unions didn't want women in their unions, and didn't want the women to unionize, because they thought that women would accept lower wages and undermine their efforts. They thought of women's work as something women did until they got married, so what mattered was what a man earned as breadwinner. In reality, many women were their children's sole support, and married women worked, too, because of a husband's injury, for instance. (There was no sick pay or unemployment insurance.) Conditions in the factories were deplorable—women in the mills breathed in cotton fluff all day, for example, and the machines were often unguarded. Accidents were frequent and there was no compensation. Overseers bullied the women or demanded sex with the threat of dismissal. The women had to learn to combine, to find the skills and the courage to work for what they needed, and to put up with disappointment and humiliation—but they kept on because the struggle was "not for ourselves alone," but for the children and the future.

Black women, both poor and middle class, had to wage an even harder struggle. They often had to organize separately because white women would not accept them—sometimes for the same reason the working men did not want women in the unions. White middle-class suffragists (even Susan B. Anthony) abandoned the cause of votes for black women because they feared to lose the support of southern white women's organizations in the fight to gain the vote. They thought that getting the vote must eventually help *all* women, but it was a bitter experience for black women.

The work of Jane Addams was a point where many kinds of thinking and organizing met. As an educated, middle-class white woman, she was at first naïve in her understanding of social realities and was a bit of a "do-gooder," but she and her friends were trying to work not only for, but with, women in the Chicago slums.

Hull House, the old mansion they bought, was in the midst of a district mainly of immigrants, people displaced by poverty and war, isolated in American culture. Jane and the others who worked with her tried to create a place where people could be at home, a place to meet, to organize, to study. They tried to encourage immigrants to take pride in the customs and crafts they had brought from their old homes and that were despised in the new country. Hull House did not break down class divisions, but, on the one hand, it gave very poor people and women especially the space, security, and confidence to confront injustice and begin to demand change. On the other hand, it gave middle-class women exposure to the realities of an unjust society and a chance to break out of traditional women's roles. For all its limitations, Hull House was a catalyst for change in the status of women.

In these and in so many ways the women's movement fought for opportunities, liberties, education, and political power such as men had. Inevitably there was a backlash, similar to the backlash more recently against the changes in the roles and attitudes of women. Those earlier feminists, too, were labeled selfish, anti-men, anti-family. They were told they were stubborn, aggressive (qualities admired in men), and, of course, unfeminine and also "unnatural," meaning lesbian.

What these women achieved, through it all, was an entry into the male world. Equality with men, to do the things men did, was the goal. It was only when that had become nearer, had in a measure been achieved, that some women—with the vote, with jobs and earnings at least comparable to those of men—began to question the goal, to question the values inherent in a male-created and male-dominated society. They began to question the assumptions that seemed to direct the world—the sacredness of profit, the urge to more and more domination, the exploitation of other humans and of the Earth's resources because only what makes money has value. For instance, it was not until quite recently, and partially, that any work *not paid for in money* was counted in the gross national product of any nation. Such work had and mostly still has *no value* in such calculations, although when it is counted, unpaid work is actually the greater part of the work in the world, and often the most important. And, varying from one region to another, it is women worldwide who do most of this unpaid work of education, health care, food production and processing, and "social work." The mindset that ignores the value of services people render each other without pay forced women to question the value of the system they had fought so hard to enter. The experience, too, of two World Wars and their unspeakable carnage seemed to many women to be the inevitable result of that same mindset.

Women began to look for different ways of thinking, different goals. They rediscovered old stories, they listened to the traditions and values of oppressed people such as Native Americans, they listened to the warnings of scientists about what mindless exploitation was doing to the Earth. Whom does all this benefit? Who profits? They still asked, as they had done earlier, What must we do to save our home, our family place? But now they also asked, What must we do to save our *Earth*, which is our only home?

Gradually, there emerged a different feminist agenda with a different vision. The earlier feminists had expected that when women had the vote and political and social power, society would change, the world would become peaceful and just and more compassionate. It didn't. Women operating in a male world, in male styles, did gain some individual freedoms—better wages, the right to divorce, to custody, to redress from harassment, and so on. But as time went on more women—and more and more men too—realized that goals of reconciliation between peoples, and between people and land, couldn't be attained by operating within the existing system—because that system was *developed* in order to conquer, to control, to exploit, whether by military means or by economic and political ones.

Some women began to develop a different kind of feminism, a feminism with a strong spiritual element—though not necessarily religious, because many felt that the big, organized religions had become part of the oppressive systems their founders had originally rejected. Something called "ecofeminism" began to emerge, seeing the exploitation of women, of the Earth, as the result of the same kind of system. Many feminists identified with the peace movement, gave leadership to it, and often suffered for it. The thrust of feminism was less toward women's rights and more toward the creation of community, at every level of scale. Public policy, they said, was to be concerned with the well-being of all society, not only of corporations, and the well-being of society depended on the well-being of the planet.

All that sounds very theoretical. Let's look at what it means on the ground. In Bangladesh, women famously prevented the destruction of the hilly forests on which the life of their communities depended by simply hugging trees and refusing to let go when men turned up with chain saws. In the end they won not only the safety of forests (and of the valleys, too, that would have been flooded and silted up when the eroded hills could not absorb the rains), but made the government rethink the policy of wholesale logging. In Africa women had always been the main farmers until "development" counted only the men as recipients of subsidies, seeds, and chemicals. In many places African women turned their skills to reclaiming arid land. They built low walls along the contours of hills to catch the rain, planting millions of tree seedlings, reclaiming hundreds of thousands of acres and making them fertile.

In many lands and places it was women who led the protests against contamination of land and water, organized to demand banning of toxic chemicals. Women wanted to save their homes and families and knew it could only be done by profound changes in the way trading, farming, and manufacturing were controlled.

All of this was, and is, about sacred place. From the home to the neighborhood to the Earth, *places* are where people live, physically, socially, spiritually. *Places* are where people learn to know one another and the Earth on which they depend—they put down roots, in many senses. This doesn't mean people shouldn't move to new places. It does mean that when the profits of corporations demand that families and whole neighborhoods be uprooted, that many be deprived of employment, that land be rendered barren, whole ecosystems destroyed and food routinely soused with toxic chemicals, then the relationships between people and place is destroyed. People and places become mere parts of the economic machine, disposable as any spare part.

This is not just about women, of course, though women have been leaders in the effort to halt the destruction and desecration of the sacred place. It is about the whole community of humans and Earth. "Place" is both cosmic in its meaning yet very particular and local.

In the Andean region of South America, the peasant peoples have evolved over many, many generations a system of agriculture that links the land and the people, who are constantly aware of the sacred land and the spirits that give it, and the humans, life. Every field is different and sacred, every operation of the farming year is accompanied by ritual. It is immensely productive and varied. There are at least 800 kinds of potato, for instance, suitable for the varied heights above sea level, degrees and kinds of fertility, the way the particular field faces, and so on. This sort of thing is anathema to developers, who prefer a market where the same seeds, the same machinery, and the same chemicals can be sold all over one region, and all farming is done in the same way. The developers tried and left, at least in many places, after disastrous failures whose abandoned machinery littered the land; weeds swallowed up failed crops.

A group of men and women from that region, who were from the first generation of these people to go to university, at first were determined to help their people by teaching them "modern" methods so they could be more productive. It took many years and failed efforts to convince them that what they were trying to do was destructive. In the end, with courage and humility, they set themselves instead to learn from their own people, to "accompany" them, as they said, and to find ways to teach others about these traditional, and very successful, ways. They struggled for years, but eventually they persuaded some of the universities to offer courses in "peasant" agriculture. And the root of all this was the awareness of the sacredness of the place.

We think of sacred place mostly in connection with shrines, cathedrals, churches, and temples, and indeed the rituals of consecration do designate centers of sacredness that are important for us, but in fact this kind of consecration often happens because the place is *already* regarded as sacred, for instance, because a holy person died in that place, or some revelation was received, as at Lourdes. Many European cathedrals were built on the sites of places already regarded as sacred by the pagan religions that were there before. Sacredness is not imposed by human decision; rather our consecration recognizes what God has made inherently sacred, and that means all of creation. Part of the feminist vision of land and people recognizes this sacredness, in essence if not always in religious terms.

Rudyard Kipling, the author, was no feminist, but for him the land he loved and cherished—his specially loved place, the county of Sussex in England—was sacred. But the actual word he used to express this was *enchanted,* and he did so in a story about how the "little people" or "good people" were expelled from England, and the luck went with them. He saw the loss of enchantment as beginning with the rise of a so-called scientific attitude that despised the wisdom of country people and assigned stories of enchantment to peasants, children, and old women. In these terms our task is "re-enchantment." Enchantment, in this sense, is the awareness of a pervasive spiritual power in places—and people are *part* of place, not extra. Thus the feminist task must be not just to promote the welfare of women but to do that within the context of the recovery of sacredness in the human places, a "re-enchantment" that treats *all* reality with awe, aware that every place—home, neighborhood, city, nation—consists of a truly awesome complexity of relationships that stretches to infinity. This is the reality of divinity, of divine presence, in all the cosmos; yet we can only truly know it in *particular* places that are *our* places.

Women who hugged trees, women who kept vigil for the "disappeared," women who organize neighborhoods to get better housing, or street lights, or garbage collection, women who *sing* as they march together, women who gather to resist church oppression, women who choose organic food for their families (even if it costs more because the government subsidizes chemical farming): all of these are engaged in the task of re-enchantment, because they are working to re-establish the deep exchanges of life, to unblock the flow of the spirit between people, between people and land.

This is the task of feminism now—to restore sacredness in places, to re-consecrate, to re-enchant. Within that, all this is good for women too. It's a huge task—but what we need to remember is that it is about restoring the true nature of created being, which is desecrated by fear, hatred, war, exploitation. It is truly the work of God that we are called to do.

5.

Feminist Theology, Catholicism, and the Family

Lisa Sowle Cahill

What is feminism and what does it have to do with theology? Why is a feminist theology important for Catholicism today? And what implications does such a theology have for the Catholic Christian view of family life?[1]

To some, "feminism" and "Catholicism" might seem to be oppositional terms. After all, they might argue, the Catholic Church denies ordination to women and portrays motherhood and domesticity as women's most important roles. Feminism, to the contrary, defends the equality of women and men in all spheres of life, and portrays the expectation that women fulfill maternal and domestic roles above all others as setting unfair limits on women's capacities and fulfillment. How can feminism and theology come together? And don't they lead to opposing views of family life, especially as far as the roles of women are concerned?

Feminist theology aims to change relationships in church and society. The project of feminist theology is to reach back into Bible and Christian tradition, and to draw on the experiences of women of faith today, in order to show that the essential faith of Christians, following the example of Jesus Christ and of his first disciples, is liberating and not oppressive for women. Although it is true that there are oppressive strands in scripture, theological teaching, and church practice, these can be contrasted to and even overcome by other strands affirming women's faith witness and our practical equality with men as members of the believing community and of society. A key meaning of Christian faith is the inclusion of the outcast and the marginalized in a community of reciprocal compassion and service. This community is the "kingdom of God" preached by Jesus or the "body of Christ" proclaimed by Paul.

Christian community as inclusive community has implications for the structure and role of Christian families. First of all, family relations should be characterized by mutuality and respect, with no hierarchy of men over women. Second, Christian families must reach out to others in a spirit of service. They should form their members to be transformative agents in cultures of materialism, competition, or violence. Christian families do not exist only to form their own members in internal relations of love or even spirituality, but also and equally to help give Christian faith and love expression and power in the world.

This message of feminist theology for women's roles and for families is truly prophetic. In fact, in the past, traditional Christian religious images and doctrines of God have not always reflected women's experiences of God or encouraged women's faith. Instead, they have reinforced unequal patterns of gender relations in society by making men seem closer to God than women. For example, Christians persistently refer to God as "Father," even though we also teach theologically that this is a metaphor and that God has no gender. The Bible includes female images of God as a mother and as Lady Wisdom or the divine Sophia. (On this point, see Elizabeth Johnson's eloquent *She Who Is: The Mystery of God in Feminist Theological Discourse.*[2]) Although the creation story in Genesis 1 tells us that men and women are made equally in God's image, the creation story in Genesis 2 is often misinterpreted to make women merely "derivative" from men, even though up until the creation of woman, the creatures made by God have appeared in ascending order of importance! Gender hierarchy does not enter the picture until after the fall (Genesis 3), where it is obviously the result of sin, and not part of the design of creation.

The leadership of women in the New Testament is also usually downplayed. The role model for women, especially Catholic women, is Mary the mother of Jesus, portrayed as the "handmaiden" of the Lord. Yet her own son tells his disciples that Mary is not to be honored for being a mother, but because she has faith and does the will of God (Luke 8:19–21). More important, there are women of faith in the New Testament who are important disciples and leaders in the churches. Paul's epistles mention many such women, including Phoebe, Chloe, Prisca, and Junia. Above all others is the example of Mary Magdalene. A distorting, misogynist tradition that confines women to sexual roles and tells us that they are inferior to men hands on the story that Mary Magdalene was a prostitute, even that her claim to fame was being in love with or a lover of Jesus (Luke 8:2). The New Testament has no such story line. Instead, it says that Jesus drove seven demons (of unspecified nature and effects) from Mary, and she became a disciple of Jesus. All four Gospels portray her as the first witness to the resurrection. Because John's Gospel records her as being sent by Jesus to share the news with the apostles, Bernard of Clairvaux termed her "the apostle to the apostles."

On the other hand, we cannot deny that parts of the New Testament itself seem to downplay the culturally unusual and religiously prophetic role that Jesus seems to have established for his women followers. Most problematic are the so-called household codes that appear in epistles written largely by followers of Paul, in his name, after his death (Col 3:18–4:1; Eph 5:21–6:9; 1 Peter 2:18–3:7; 1 Tim 2:18–15; Titus 2:1–10, 3:1). These sets of instruction reflect ancient Greek codes of "household management," and may have been created by the early church to dilute the subversive effect of Christian conversion on familial and social behavior, in order to gain acceptance for what was viewed by some as a dangerous new cult. The household codes command women to be submissive to their husbands, slaves to their masters, and children to their parents, though they also advise men to treat subordinates kindly and to love their wives. The power, however, is obviously on the men's side.

Interestingly, official Catholic teaching has never approached these texts in a literal or fundamentalist sense. Although Catholicism has certainly joined the rest of Western culture in treating women as though we need male guidance and control, recent Catholic teaching shows the impact of feminist criticism and the actual greater social equality of women. An example of this is the way the problem of a supposedly Bible-based theory of male "headship" is treated in papal teaching. John Paul II does not assert the authority of men over women in the family. Instead, he uses categories evoking equality, equal dignity, reciprocity, and mutuality to describe the relation of spouses. A favorite description of the ideal spousal relationship is "mutual self-gift."

In his 1981 treatise *On the Family,* John Paul II insists, "It is important to underline the equal dignity and responsibility of women with men." He explains that "this equality is realized in a unique manner in that reciprocal self-giving by each to the other and by both to the children which is proper to marriage and the family."[3] In a letter written in 1995, preparing for the United Nations' Fourth World Conference on Women in Beijing, the pope notes past and present injustices to women. He expresses admiration for women who have fought for "their basic social, economic and political rights," even in times when this was considered "a lack of femininity, a manifestation of exhibitionism, and even a sin!" He refers to "the great process of women's liberation," and voices regret that women are still often not "acknowledged, respected and appreciated."[4]

It may be true, as many feminist theologians have pointed out, that the ideal of male-female equality is undermined by the pope's insistence that motherhood is the primary feminine vocation, and by the exclusion of women from priestly ministry. However, it is also true that John Paul II has defended the equality and rights of women in the family and in society to an extent far exceeding the teaching of previous pontiffs.

There are at least three factors that explain the pope's position on women and his nonendorsement of a "headship" model of the family. First, it should be noted that he does not favor a liberal feminism focused on autonomy. Rather, in accord with Catholic social teaching, he adopts a social view of the person. In this view, all have a right to share equally in the common good, but rights and duties are reciprocal and interdependent. Also, different roles can be appropriate for different people without violating the basic principle of equality. Regarding women, John Paul II sees motherhood as their special role, without granting that this places women in a submissive position in relation to men. Second, and related to this, is the pope's strong "preferential option for the poor," an approach to social ethics in which the vulnerable and marginalized are given special attention. In many cultures of the world, and in some aspects of all societies, it is taken for granted that women are the social inferiors of men, and hence are deprived of full participation in the common good. Thus the pope advocates for women's dignity, along with that of other vulnerable groups.

Third, the Catholic approach to theology and conduct has never been based on a literal or fundamentalist interpretation of the Bible. The Bible is an important authority for Catholic theology, but it is interpreted in relation to its own historical context, to complementary and mutually correcting themes within the Bible as a whole, to church traditions of theology and practice, and to contemporary needs and insights. Thus biblical references to "submission" and "headship" do not become red flags or litmus tests for Catholic identity in the way that they do in some Protestant denominations. (There is such a thing as "Catholic fundamentalism," but it is much more likely to focus on papal encyclicals and on Vatican decrees than on scriptural proof-texts.)

Let us examine each of these points in turn.

The Person, the Common Good, and Women's Roles

In the one hundred-year-old tradition of social encyclicals, the "common good" is a central concept. A representative statement comes from the 1963 encyclical of Pope John XXIII, *Peace on Earth*.[5] "Since men [and women] are social by nature they are meant to live with others and to work for one another's welfare."[6] Further, "the very nature of the common good requires that all members of the political community be entitled to share in it, although in different ways according to each one's tasks, merits and circumstances." However, "justice and equity" can sometimes mandate that society and civil government "give more attention to the less fortunate members of the community, since they are less able to defend their rights and to assert their legitimate claims."[7] As long as thirty-five years ago, John XXIII realized that "women are taking a part in public life," "becoming ever more conscious of their human dignity," and thus "demand rights befitting a human person both in domestic and in public life."[8] John Paul II speaks more specifically of the equality of the sexes, similarly defending women's "rights and role within family and society."[9] He endorses "personal rights" and "real equality in every area," including "equality of spouses with regard to family rights."[10]

Specifically on the family, the pope considers women's role as mother to have a special value, and even to manifest par excellence the "special genius of women."[11] Nonetheless, he does not limit women's place to the domestic sphere. Instead, he criticizes "a widespread social and cultural tradition" about "family life" that "has considered women's role to be exclusively that of wife and mother, without adequate access to public functions, which have generally been reserved for men." He insists, "There is no doubt that the equal dignity and responsibility of men and women fully

justifies women's access to public functions." Proper education will guarantee that "discrimination between the different types of work and professions is eliminated at its very
root," the "image of God in man and woman" being thereby
illumined.[12] In his letter for Beijing, John Paul expresses
thanks not only to wives, mothers, and members of religious
communities, but adds, "Thank you women who work! You
are present and active in every area of life—social, economic,
cultural, artistic and political."[13]

All this does not mean, however, that the pope sees
women and men as *identical* in personality, gifts, or roles.
Although women should have access to virtually all the social
roles open to men, they will exercise these roles in different
ways. John Paul II is a proponent of *complementary* gender
characteristics, although not necessarily separate social roles.
Clearly, this viewpoint helps retain a base in Catholic teaching for the exclusion of women from the ministerial priest-
hood.[14] Yet it also promotes respect for women who exercise
the vocation of mother and remain in the home. The pope
finally sees the parental roles of mother and father as coop-
erative and reciprocal, even suggesting that men "learn"
fatherhood from women, whose experiences of pregnancy
and birth enhance their predisposition "of paying attention *to
another person*."[15] A feminist critique may fault the idea that
women are inherently more sensitive to others than men,
because it consigns both sexes to constraining gender stereo-
types and results ultimately in more passive and subordinate
roles for women. Nevertheless, the pope explicitly rejects "a

wrong superiority of male prerogatives which humiliates women and inhibits the development of healthy family relationships."[16]

Injustice toward Women and the Christian Response

As a matter of historical fact, women have been subordinated to men, and this is a grave injustice. John Paul II, on behalf of the church and Christian tradition, even takes some responsibility for this situation. Women "have often been relegated to the margins of society and even reduced to servitude....And if objective blame...has belonged to not just a few members of the church, for this I am truly sorry."[17] He mentions many examples, among them sexual violence, the prostitution of young girls, and the complicity of men and "the general social environment" in pressuring women into abortions.[18]

To formulate a Christian response, John Paul II adopts the special stance of support toward powerless groups that has uniformly marked his encyclical letters, for example, *The Gospel of Life* (1995). Jesus of Nazareth "proclaims to all who feel threatened and hindered that their lives too are a good to which the Father's love gives meaning and value."[19]

> When it comes to setting women free from every kind of exploitation and domination, the Gospel contains an ever relevant message which goes back to the attitude of Jesus Christ himself. Transcending

the established norms of his own culture, Jesus treated women with openness, respect, acceptance and tenderness. In this way he honored the dignity which women have always possessed according to God's plan and in his love. As we look to Christ at the end of this second millennium, it is natural to ask ourselves how much of his message has been heard and acted upon.[20]

The pope follows the tradition of modern Catholic social teaching by affirming a standard of justice as social equality and participation in the common good, then taking the Bible as an authority in establishing a special commitment to work for the "poor." This category includes all those who suffer unjust discrimination and exclusion for any reason. The example of Jesus is specifically used to show that women in general, though to a greater or lesser degree in varying cultural situations, belong in the category of those deserving of affirmative, inclusive social support.

Biblical Interpretation

In this spirit, John Paul interprets particular biblical passages about the roles of women and men, and about marriage and family. An important example is his treatment of Paul's "Letter to the Ephesians," chapter 5, where marriage is compared to the relation of Christ and church. This text is the standard source of the concept of "headship," since in it

Paul compares the love of husband for wife to that of Christ for the church, then adds that the husband is head of the wife, just as Christ is head of the church. The pope devotes a full chapter of *Vocation of Women* to Ephesians' "bride and bridegroom" metaphor without ever bringing up the topic of "headship." The main point developed by the pope in this chapter is not the hierarchy of the sexes in marriage (an idea that is denied), but the permanent faithfulness of love in marriage, a faithfulness premised precisely on the mutuality and equality of the spouses. Men's loyalty to family ties need not and should not be purchased at the price of women's subordination to men's choices and demands. Both marriage and parenthood are the mutual, shared responsibilities of men and women. The recognition of the mutuality that properly characterizes marriage is dawning only gradually "in hearts, consciences, behavior and customs." Making equal, mutual, and faithful love a reality in marriage is a challenge to human history comparable in the pope's view to the abolition of slavery.[21]

A concrete application of this view of women, marriage, and family is the pope's rejection of all violence against women, in any circumstances. Following his lead, our own U.S. bishops authored a pastoral letter on domestic violence in 1992 titled "When I Call for Help."[22] They state unequivocally that no biblical text about the submission of women can serve as an excuse for domestic abuse or justify advice to women to remain with abusing husbands or partners. Going even farther, the bishops tell churches and counselors that they must assist women to leave abusive situations immediately and provide abusers a mandate and support to change their behavior. Violence against women or in the household is never justified.

The pope does maintain that women and men have different "masculine" and "feminine" personalities, though he does not interpret this complementarity as hierarchy, either in society or in marriage. A question or problem created by the pope's definition of women and men as "different but equal" is whether the centrality that John Paul II attributes to motherhood in defining the feminine personality results in an imbalance in male and female roles, insofar as women are more responsible for children and less available for other social roles. Likewise, men's participation in the family is not equally encouraged and respected.

This results in inequality, in that male and female spheres of activity are both limited in stereotypical ways. Moreover, "women's sphere" is socially less valued; and the preeminence of women even in the domestic realm is compromised by the economic dependence of most women and children "in the family" on men. These are all consequences that the pope wants to avoid. The dependency and inequality of women would be exacerbated still further if men were granted authority over women even in what is supposedly women's own special sphere of competence; this is a move from which John Paul II distances himself. But the compatibility of complementarity and equality in defining gender roles needs further reflection and discussion.

Families

Feminists have frequently criticized the "public-private split" that characterizes the modern "nuclear" family. The nuclear unit of mother-father-children is actually a recent development and is not the "traditional" family form. In most traditional societies, parents and children coexist within the extended family, and one's birth family is often more important to one's identity than the family one forms by marriage. Moreover, women's and men's work is not always so strictly separated by location into domestic and public spaces. Feminism in North America frequently has taken a "liberal" social and political form, advocating for women's equality in entering the traditional male work sphere. More recently, feminists, especially those from other cultural traditions, are calling attention to the need for different work and family arrangements, permitting both women and men access to both public and domestic types of work and vocations.

The pope's general perspective on social ethics greatly influences his view of the institution of family, and hence his approach to the relations of men and women in that institution. The pope understands every person as inherently social and does not portray families as "nuclear" units only, but as participating in and contributing to the common good by fulfilling many social roles. His perspective on families is social and global, and, as always, he is very sensitive to economic patterns of injustice that exemplify domination of the weak by the strong. He is thus aware of the injustices to women that can distort family relations. Respect for the equality of women becomes part of the preferential option for the poor.

Moreover, the family as a whole should model commitment to the common good. Certainly most would agree that the situation of family life in our culture presents Christian disciples with many challenges. How can a Christian family live out its faith in the world? The Catholic response, at least in part, is that Christian family virtues are realized in the process of living out faith in the world as a "preferential option for the poor." Christian discipleship criticizes models of family that are focused on individual self-fulfillment, that use family welfare as a rationalization for indifference to less fortunate families, or that internalize in family structures the materialist, violent, or dominating relationships present in the culture. On the other hand, Christian discipleship appropriates and builds on natural bonds of spouses, parents and children, and extended families, transforming family love and commitment toward inclusion of "neighbors" in need. Gender equality in the family teaches an important lesson for the way we approach those outside our families.

The documents of Vatican II and the writings of John Paul II both reflect this positive, activist, and humanitarian posture toward discipleship when they treat marriage and family. The Catholic vision of family has developed even since the council's *Gaudium et Spes,* especially in terms of the breadth of its vision of families, its awareness of the complex relations between nuclear families and their social settings, its sensitivity to the plight of the world's oppressed, and certainly in its view of the mutuality of the sexes in marriage. These trends are present in the writings of John Paul II (e.g., *Familiaris Consortio*, nos. 44, 18–20). Yet *Gaudium et Spes* sounds the keynote for subsequent teaching, especially the metaphor of family as "domestic church": "The family is a kind of school of deeper humanity" (no. 52; see also nos. 25, 26 on the common good). Citing this characterization, and reflecting its augmentation by Christian ideals, John Paul II expands in *Familiaris Consortio:* "This happens where there is care and love for the little ones, the sick, the aged; where there is mutual service every day; when there is a sharing of goods, of joys and of sorrows" (no. 21). Above all, we need to revive and reinvigorate the Catholic model of family as a locus of social responsibility in our individualist, libertarian, and morally relativist culture (cf. Evangelicum Vitae, nos. 4, 20). The credibility of our message about families will also depend on the continuing expansion of the theme of gender equality, a much stronger note in current papal writings than in centuries (and even decades) past (FC, nos. 22–25), but one that will still require amplification through the contributions of feminist theologians.

Notes

1. This essay was prepared for publication in 2001, some four-and-a-half years after it was delivered as a lecture. The approach of the final version is to examine feminist critiques of Catholic theology, especially as related to gender and family, and to show how recent Catholic, especially papal, teaching has been affected by feminist insights. It also outlines

some remaining problems in the papal view of women's roles in the family, thus indicating the need for continuing feminist analysis.

2. Elizabeth A. Johnson, *She Who Is: The Mystery of God in Feminist Theological Discourse* (New York: Crossroad, 1992).

3. John Paul II, *On the Family* (Washington, DC: United States Catholic Conference, 1981), no. 22.

4. John Paul II, *Letter to Women,* June 29, l995, no. 6 (published on the Internet by Catholic Resource Network, Trinity Communications, P.O. Box 3610, Manassas, VA 22110/CRNET.ORG). Also published by the United States Catholic Conference, Washington, DC.

5. John XXIII, *Peace on Earth,* in William J. Gibbons, S.J., *Seven Great Encyclicals* (New York/Paramus: Paulist Press, 1963), 289–335.

6. Ibid., no. 31.

7. Ibid., no. 56.

8. Ibid., no. 41.

9. *On the Family,* no. 22.

10. *Letter to Women,* no. 4.

11. *On the Dignity and Vocation of Women* (Washington, DC: United States Catholic Conference: 1988), nos. 30–31; *Letter to Women,* nos. 9–11.

12. Ibid., no. 23.

13. *Letter to Women,* no. 2.

14. Ibid., nos. 7, 11.

15. *Vocation of Women,* no. 18.

16. *On the Family,* no. 25.

17. *Letter to Women,* no. 3.

18. Ibid., no. 5.

19. John Paul II, *The Gospel of Life* (Boston: Pauline Books, 1995), no. 32.

20. *Letter to Women,* no. 3.

21. *Vocation of Women,* no. 24.

22. U.S. Bishops' Committee on Women in Society and in the Church and Committee on Marriage and Family Life, "When I Call for Help: A Pastoral Response to Domestic Violence," *Origins* 22 (November 1992): 353, 355–58.

6.

Fixing Public Schools: A Catholic Feminist Analysis

Christine E. Gudorf

On the topic of public education, there is an interesting overlap of Catholic and feminist approaches. Media presentations of feminism as a radical challenge to the church because of issues such as reproductive rights and women's ordination have made it easy to lose sight of the fact that on the majority of social issues there are few differences between feminism and Catholic teaching. Both are acutely aware of continuing victimization of millions by poverty and class, race and ethnicity, sex and age, and other factors that make for powerlessness and marginalization in our world. Both international feminism and Catholic social teaching express a moral commitment to equal dignity and well-being of each and every person and to the elimination of attitudes and conditions that support unnecessary suffering and unequal access to resources.

Contemporary Catholic social teaching and international feminism both represent movement beyond earlier, more parochial, self-interested stances of the U.S. church and the women's movement. In the American church, nativist attacks on the church precipitated the limitation of concern to problems and institutions internal to the church, especially Catholic schools. The same temptation to focus on narrow self-interest led many in the early women's movement to either ignore the struggles of other groups or to project their own white middle-class issues and struggles onto women in general. But ongoing participation of both U.S. bishops and U.S. white middle-class feminists in dialogues and projects with other diverse domestic groups, as well as with their Third World counterparts, have corrected and broadened originally more narrow foci and commitments. Those dialogues and joint projects are sometimes warm and sometimes acrimonious—the true nature of fraternal and sororial relations.

Feminism is both a perspective that insists on the equality of women with men and a movement committed to transforming social relations toward that equality. The church has long assumed a responsibility to redress social ills and recreate or preserve the common social good. Feminism's worldview and commitment became increasingly congruent with that of Catholic teaching as the popes gradually conceded, one piece at a time, historic church teaching on the inequality of the sexes.[1] The surrender of sexual inequality took over half a century, from the pontificate of Pius XI—who argued that inequality between the sexes was "demanded by the welfare of the family and by the order and unity which must reign in the home"[2]—to those of Paul VI and John Paul II, who respectively recognized women's equal social[3] and familial[4] rights. While there are still issues between feminism and the church in the areas of reproduction and roles and governance within the church, these are relatively few compared to the similarity of approach on other issues of justice, peace, and community.

From the perspectives of both feminism and Catholic social teaching, it would be time in this nation to end the exclusion of public education from the broad range of Catholic social teaching, even if the majority of Catholic children, including at least 90 percent of Catholic high school students, were not attending public schools. But, in fact, they are.[5]

In this brief space, one can only offer preliminary reflection in hopes of stimulating further discussion. After a short survey of problems in U.S. public education, I propose a brief list of principles from both Catholic social teaching and feminism that are relevant to public education, and then proceed to an even briefer reflection on what those principles have to say about some of the educational options facing the nation.

The Crisis in Public Education Today

Different segments of society describe the crisis in public education differently, but social teaching and feminism for the most part agree: School violence, falling student achievement, segregation and resegregation, funding inequities, and the scarcity and shortage of teachers top their lists. School violence, which actually peaked in 1993, had by 1998 become a national priority, once the kids killing and being killed were no longer only black urban kids in drug-related school incidents but white rural and suburban kids as well. Between 1992 and 1998, 251 killings occurred in public schools, with many times that number wounded and traumatized. For feminists, the fact that over 90 percent of school killers are males must be one part of the analysis and addressed in proposed remedies.

Shared concern for equality in feminism and social teaching leads to concern about segregation and resegregation in public schools. White flight to both suburban public schools and private schools has left urban public schools serving a disproportionately poor and minority clientele with a high level of special needs. In some areas of the country, Catholic schools have been the recipient of white flight, though Catholic schools as a group have a student body that is 22 percent minority: 10 percent Hispanic, 9 percent African American, and 3 percent Asian.[6] Like non-minority enrollment in Catholic schools, minority enrollment is partly due to parents seeking religious education for the children, and partly due to parents fleeing with their children from dangerous schools with poor educational achievement. In some cases it is also due to minority scholarships deliberately designed to diversify the student body and thus discourage white parents from choosing parochial schools to avoid integration.

The plight of public schools is not, in general, the result of private (including Catholic) schools siphoning off more economically privileged Catholic and non-Catholic students. Between 1890 and 1995 private schools have enrolled between 7.3 percent and 13.8 percent of U.S. students. Until the 1970s, about 80 percent of private school students were in Catholic schools, and they were not the rich. As historian William Newman, citing a number of studies, writes:

> In the opening decades of the twentieth century Catholic school students were a less affluent group than public school students. And even though Catholic families moved up the nation's economic ladder as the century unfolded, Catholic schools students have never been far more advantaged than public school students.[7]

Beginning in the 1970s, Catholic schools began closing, and fundamentalist Christian schools began opening. Since the mid 1980s, 55 percent of private school students attend Catholic schools. The 15 percent who attend fundamentalist Christian schools are from mostly lower middle-class and working-class backgrounds, significantly less affluent than the public school body.[8] Thus about 70 percent of private school students are from approximately the same economic level, or even lower, as those in the public schools. The problem is not illuminated in national statistics; where great class differences loom between Catholic schools, or even private schools in general, and public schools, they are local patterns.

A number of dioceses attempted to compensate for the negative effect of white suburban Catholic schools on the availability of quality education to urban minorities by financially supporting one or more Catholic schools—invariably elementary—in urban core areas populated by minorities. But even where funding for such schools is continued, it is often inadequate, insecure—threatened annually with cancellation due to diocesan budgetary problems. This insecurity undermines the confidence of families and staff in the schools, decreasing their incentive to invest themselves in these schools, as well as undermining the possibility for long-term administrative planning. While these schools do nothing to address the residential patterns that promote resegregation, they are lifelines to some escaping from the worst of the public schools.

Another major concern is effectiveness of learning in the public schools. Feminism and social teaching both recognize adequate education as critical to human well-being and equal access to quality education as a basic social justice issue. While falling achievement has been a popular concern for decades now, it is difficult to assess to what extent achievement has fallen. The fact that is clearest is that the consequences of lack

117

of educational achievement have become drastically more negative. When significant parts of the workforce lacked a high school diploma, limited ability to read was a handicap in steady employment, but not an insurmountable one. But when a majority of the workforce has post-secondary training of some kind, functional illiteracy usually dooms an individual in many areas of life. Without literacy, one cannot fill out employment forms or conduct the daily chores of living, such as operate a checking account or credit card, respond to mail, legal summons, or notes from one's children's teachers, much less teach one's own children to read. So although many parts of the country have lower high school dropout rates than half a century before, the children the schools fail to reach suffer more than in the past. And in some parts of the nation, especially large urban centers, functional illiteracy and dropout rates have actually increased.

Historians point out that the 1950s—now often regarded as the apex of educational achievement in public schools—actually produced the first wave of exposés of ineffective public schools, including Rudolph Flesch's *Why Johnny Can't Read* (1955), Arthur Bestor's *Educational Wastelands* (1953), and Mortimer Smith's *The Diminished Mind* (1954).[9] Today some states have begun to require statewide exams of high school students to determine graduation, and many have found the results shocking. More than 10 percent of Florida high school seniors, given three and then even four tries to pass a test set at sixth to eighth grade reading and math levels, still fail.[10] Sometimes the efforts of the schools to have students succeed in statewide testing are as shocking as the proportion of failures. In 1997–1998, Riverside Elementary School in Miami was faced with the possibility of testing for the third consecutive year onto a statewide list of "Worst" achieving schools, and thus at risk of being forcibly reorganized, including teacher and principal reassignments or firings. In June 1998 the *Miami Herald* told the story of how the school avoided such a fate.[11] Since in Florida, as in many other states, an elementary school's ranking is based only on the reading and math scores of fourth graders, all the teacher aides and specialist teachers were stripped from all the other grades and given to the fourth grade. All teachers were required to volunteer for a two-hour after-school tutoring program for fourth graders, and all subjects except for reading and math were stripped from the fourth grade curriculum. Finally, large numbers of poor readers in the fourth grade were referred to special education classes because test scores of special education students were not averaged in with the rest of the fourth graders. In 1997–1998, 27 of 42 kids in Riverside's special education program were fourth graders. With the help of all these measures, Riverside's test scores rose, and it escaped the "Worst" list. Neither feminism nor social teaching could justify this diversion of resources, since it was not based on assessments of individual student need.

Some states test teachers as well. In 1998 only 60 percent of Massachusetts's public school teachers passed a basic skills test.[12] Some states encourage teachers to earn certification at the national level. Beginning in 1998, Iowa offered any teacher who earned national board certification a bonus of $50,000—$10,000 a year for five years.[13] The program quickly produced six times the number of certified teachers the legislature had anticipated, which caused the legislature to first cut the awards by 50 percent and then to phase them out altogether. Many districts employ significant numbers of teachers who do not meet state certification levels. New York City lowered the number of uncertified teachers from 1 in 2 to 1 in 4 over the last three years, and is struggling with recent court decisions that prevent placing any uncertified teachers in those schools whose performance is the lowest. While the court order has been met at the elementary level by sending virtually all the newly hired certified elementary teachers into the poorest performing schools, the rights of senior teachers to a say in placements has prevented replacing many uncertified teachers in middle and high schools.[14] The previous education administration offered 15 percent bonuses to certified teachers willing to volunteer in the poorest schools but without significant response; studies indicated that it would take about a $20,000 differential to attract well-qualified teachers to the poorest schools. Two community school districts in Brooklyn, New York, offer teacher and principal bonuses to the schools most successful in raising student reading and math scores. In June 2001, eight Brooklyn schools earned bonuses that ranged from $2,000 per teacher and $15,000 per principal to $1,000 for teachers and $5,000 for principals.[15] In California, a new program introduced in 1999 to offer rewards to schools and educators for improvements in student performance resulted in 71 percent of 6,800 participating schools meeting their targets.[16] One thousand teachers received $25,000 each, followed by 3,750 who received $10,000 and 7,500 receiving $5,000, and the successful schools themselves split $175 million. The size of the awards depended upon the size of the gains.

In some places, teacher shortages are so acute that signing bonuses to attract teachers from other areas, rather than bonuses based on achievement, are the order of the day. Ft. Worth, Texas, has offered a signing bonus of $5,200, most commonly used as the down payment on a house. Since instituting the program, Ft. Worth has filled its vacancies with teachers from surrounding states and counties.[17] Similar programs, some modeled on that of Ft. Worth, have sprung up in Massachusetts, Ohio, and California, as well as in other states.

The teacher shortage is not merely a matter of salaries, though that is one key issue. There is a sharp disparity in most states between the per pupil funding level in poor and middle-class school districts. There are still school districts in which per pupil funding is less than $3,000, and some where per pupil funding exceeds $20,000. Across the nation as a whole, teacher salaries are significantly below levels of thirty and forty years ago in terms of purchasing power. And in the many urban districts there are not sufficient funds to maintain and renovate the stock of aging buildings. Most districts have increased administrative and staff hiring at higher rates than teacher hiring, at least partly in response to intensified reporting requirements by monitoring agencies.

On the topic of teacher salaries and skill levels: my husband and I had undergraduate degrees in education, specifically secondary social studies. We were two of the top ten scholastic achievers in our 1967 high school graduating class. Among those top ten students (two National Merit Finalists), one went into nursing, one into pre-law, and eight into education. We saw that our rural Indiana teachers were not only relatively dedicated, but also were able to support a non-working spouse, own a house and a car or two, and save for their children's college educations. Today, in much of the nation, the salary of a beginning teacher with a non-working spouse and two children is below the poverty line, and home ownership is out of the question without a working spouse who earns at least as much. Even a couple where both are teachers must often choose between home ownership and college savings for their children.

When we took education courses in the late '60s, it was common to poke fun at the introductory courses—much of the content and method taught seemed so simple and commonsensical. But the humor over education has changed. Today the faculty and students at U.S. colleges and universities are not just poking fun at education courses, but at education students. "What can you expect—he's an education major!" is a frequent refrain. Comparison of average grades on required core (non-major) courses between groups of majors (business, education, history, math, English, nursing, psychology, physics, engineering, and other disciplines) routinely finds education majors at or near the very bottom.

These are, of course, only averages. There continue to be very bright young people who choose education as a career, and the schools still have bright, dedicated teachers in their ranks. But the ratio has changed a great deal. It is virtually unheard of today that top students in any academic field become grade or high school teachers. They go into business, engineering, computer science, medicine, research science, and law. Many of my best students who would like to become teachers say they can't: they would have to postpone marriage and live with their parents for years in order to be able both to live and to pay back expensive bank and government education loans on a teacher's salary. For students who graduate with $25,000–$40,000 in education loans, the prospect of beginning salaries in the low to mid-twenties and a job that requires them to earn a graduate degree within a very few years puts education outside the realm of realistic choices.

Feminism has also hurt education indirectly by opening other professional careers to women. I have nieces in medical school, engineering school, law school, and completing doctorates in anthropology and management—all of whose mothers thought nursing and teaching were the only post-college career paths open to women. Just as the Catholic schools long benefited from the low-paid labor of Catholic nuns, the public schools benefited from the comparatively low-paid labor of the brightest female minds in the nation, because there were few other attractive career options open to them.

Christine E. Gudorf

Current Proposals

In response to these widely recognized problems, there are a number of current proposals. One proposal is vouchers, in which the parents of each eligible school-age child receive a voucher good for the cost of educating one child in the public schools for one year. The parents could present that voucher to the school of their choice,[18] which the school could then cash like a check.

A few states have provisions for charter schools. A charter school is a school that has been organized by a group or institution and that becomes publicly funded by having its charter approved by the state and local boards of education. The school is responsible for meeting the goals of the charter, which include the attainment of general educational standards. The defenders of both vouchers and charter schools argue that in addition to providing the quality education that many public schools are not, vouchers and charter schools would provide the competition that could revitalize public schools. Catholic bishops have been more enthusiastic about vouchers, since most but not all charter proposals have excluded "sectarian" schools. On the other hand, the two functioning voucher programs (in Minnesota and Ohio) that include religious schools are defending that inclusion in court. Under a voucher system, Catholic parents could use vouchers to send their children to Catholic schools. This would take the funding of Catholic schools off the backs of parents, parishes, and dioceses. Ultimately, however, the inclusion of Catholic schools in either charter or voucher programs will have to survive court tests involving not only the First Amendment in general, but specific issues such as prayer in schools as well.

Principles of Catholic Social Teaching

Catholic social teaching as a specific body of documents is only slightly more than a century old, beginning with Leo XIII's *Rerum Novarum* in 1891, though many of the principles and concepts in social teaching have a much longer history in church teaching. The first social teaching document focused on justice between employers and employees; successive documents greatly expanded that focus to include justice in the economic relations of rich and poor nations and justice for a variety of poor and marginalized groups: migrants, women and children, native peoples, the poor and victims of violence. Within Catholic social teaching, we find both general foundational principles that apply to all social institutions and specific teachings that bear on education.

General foundational principles in both social teaching and feminism[19] begin with the principle of justice, understood as giving to each person what is due him or her consistent with the dignity and equality of all persons. Other principles, such as subsidiarity, solidarity, and preferential option for the poor, help to elaborate the general principle of justice. These three principles explain different aspects of what it is that is due each and every child of God. Each of these in turn corresponds to feminist principles of justice.

The principle of "subsidiarity" is a very old principle in church teaching that far predates modern social teaching. Subsidiarity requires that decision making be done at the lowest, most inclusive level that is effective. Applying the principle of subsidiarity, recent popes beginning with Paul VI have insisted that every person in society has a right to be involved in the decision making that affects his or her life. We all have obligations with and to the larger society in which we live. Obligation is linked to responsibility. We cannot have obligations in areas in which we have not been allowed to exercise responsibility. Because women tended to be excluded from decision making in traditional societies, participation in decision making—in personal health care, in marriage and family, in careers, in social organizations and government—became a key demand in the women's movement. The slogan "The personal is political" reflected the discovery that personal experience should move social commitments because personal life is not private and unconnected to the public realm, but rather reflects a process of social construction that can be reconstructed.[20] Early feminism struggled hard to eliminate leadership elites by keeping decision making extremely inclusive, participative, and so far as possible based in consensus, and these values endure in feminist practice.

The popes have recognized that in different circumstances the appropriate level of decision making will differ. Much of nineteenth- and early twentieth-century church teaching invoked the principle of subsidiarity in protesting attempts of European states to centralize decision making, moving it farther from the local level of individual citizens. But John XXIII pointed out that the new serious worldwide problems such as pollution of the oceans demanded the creation of new levels of decision making, even higher than that of individual nations, in order to effectively deal with the problems. The appropriate— because the lowest effective—level of decision making can only be determined by investigating the specific issue within its particular context. In education, for example, it could be appropriate to have the school or district control teacher hiring, firing, and promotion at the same time that the standards for teacher certification are set by the state, region, or nation. Subsidiarity and the "the personal is political" reinforce one another here.

The principle of solidarity is a fairly recent formulation by John Paul II based on a longstanding Catholic stress on the common good. At the heart of Catholic belief is a conviction that, as the bishops wrote at Vatican II, "God intended the earth and all that it contains for the use of every human being and people. Thus, as all men [sic] follow justice and unite in charity, created goods should abound for them on a reasonable basis."[21] Paul VI quoted this in his encyclical *Populorum Progressio* and then added, "All other rights whatsoever, including those of property and free commerce, are to be subordinated to this principle."[22] John Paul II has taught in *Sollicitudo Rei Socialis* that solidarity is a "firm and persevering determination to commit oneself to the common good; that is to say to the good of all and to each individual, because we are all really responsible for all."[23] According to John Paul II, solidarity results from realizing our interdependence with others.[24] Solidarity is also a key value for feminism, for which it refers not only to solidarity among women as women, but to all denied equality and dignity and with others, including men, willing to struggle for human equality and dignity.

Another principle that supports justice is preferential option for the poor. The term "preferential option for the poor" arose within Latin American liberation theology, but John Paul has insisted that it is a foundational Christian principle elaborated both in the example of God in the Old Testament and Jesus in the New Testament. It was out of a preferential option for the poor that John Paul cried out to the Indians of Oaxaca and Chiapas, Mexico, in January 1979, "The Church is on your side." Even further, he told the Indians, "Seeing a situation that is seldom better and sometimes even worse, the pope chooses to be your voice, the voice of those who cannot speak or who have been silenced. He wishes to be the conscience of consciences, an invitation to action, to make up for lost time, which has frequently been a time of prolonged sufferings and unsatisfied hopes."[25]

The preferential option for the poor does not claim that God, or the historical Jesus, had or has an exclusive option for the poor. God loves all, and Jesus admitted diverse peoples to the group that followed him, including some nonpoor. God's choice of the Hebrew slaves and Jesus' option for the poor and marginalized of his own society were predicated upon the suffering and need of these groups. Motivated by love and compassion, God and Jesus reached out first to those in need—not because they were better or more meritorious, but because their need was greater. As their need declines, they lose priority, for the desired end, the common good, is a community without poverty and unnecessary suffering. In terms of U.S. public education, the preferential option for the poor must be for those least served, who are largely the economically poor: African Americans, Hispanics, and poor whites. Feminism, especially in the form of feminist liberation theology, concurs with this preferential option for the poor.[26]

The preferential option for the poor complements solidarity and subsidiarity, and together they give substance to justice for the common good. Preferential option for the poor and solidarity strengthen the common good by strengthening its weakest links. Subsidiarity supports the common good by insisting that ordinary poor and less powerful people be included in social decision making so that their interests are served, thus discouraging creation of a permanent poor class.

There are yet other important social teaching concepts. The just wage, for example, was elaborated by Leo XIII in *Rerum Novarum* and affirmed by every pope since. Leo defined the just wage as one that allowed a worker to fill all the basic needs of self, spouse, and children and, with thrift, to save toward ownership of private property.

It did not matter, said Leo, whether the employer and employee had agreed on a wage. If that wage did not meet these conditions, it was not just.[27] Because the individual employee does not have the power to negotiate with an employer on an equal basis, Leo supported what was in his day a controversial concept: labor unions. He argued that only by a union of employees could employees bring sufficient power to labor negotiations to protect their basic interests. Feminism also assumes the legitimacy of labor unions, and argues for equal pay for equal work. Womanists (black feminists) have conscienticized much of U.S. feminism to the understanding that feminist ethics are first of all survival ethics, thus leading to increased feminist pressure for such measures as raising the minimum wage, including childcare provision in welfare to work programs, providing more job training, equal access for women to drug programs, cleaning up toxic dumps near residential neighborhoods, and rodent eradication projects in urban areas.[28] Each of these requires education of the public in order to become enacted, and every one affects the general health and readiness of children to be taught in the public schools.

Many documents in social teaching have included references to education. In documents dealing with international development, popes and Vatican congregations have insisted that education provides access to culture, and that participation in the social and political life of a culture cannot be denied "for reasons of sex, race, color, social condition, language or religion."[29] Paul VI wrote in *Populorum Progressio* in 1967:

> Basic education is the primary object of any plan of development. Indeed, hunger for education is no less debasing than hunger for food; an illiterate person is a person with an underdeveloped mind. To be able to read and write, to acquire a professional formation, means to recover confidence in oneself and to discover that one can progress along with others.[30]

In John Paul II's *Centesimus Annus,* on the hundredth anniversary of *Rerum Novarum,* he expanded on this theme. Though primarily addressing the cities of the Third World, what he said applies equally well to many of the inner cities of our nation:

> The fact is that many people, perhaps the majority today, do not have the means which could enable them to take their place in an effective and humanly dignified way within a productive system in which work is truly central. They have no way of acquiring the basic knowledge which would enable them to express their creativity and develop their potential. They have no way of entering the network of knowledge and intercommunication which would enable them to see their qualities appreciated and utilized. Thus, if not exploited,

they are to a great extent marginalized; economic development takes place over their heads.... Allured by the dazzle of an opulence which is beyond their reach, and at the same time driven by necessity, these people crowd the cities of the Third World where they are often without cultural roots, and where they are exposed to situations of violent uncertainty, without the possibility of being integrated.[31]

References such as this point to the need for education not only to provide basic life skills, including literacy, but to provide specialized education that brings access to work and helps to ground persons in their own culture.

Applying the Principles

Principles of Catholic social teaching and of feminism deal both with the end—the kind of society at which we should aim—as well as the procedures of decision making that we utilize to reach that end. Principles must be applied in particular situations. This entails a process of analyzing the situation, deciding on specific actions, then analyzing the results of those actions in the light of the end desired. Once we analyze the results in the light of the desired end, we must decide whether to stay with the actions we chose or to modify our actions in order to better achieve our goals.

The "personal is political" motto and the principle of subsidiarity both affirm a general choice for local control of public schools. This does not mean that states, or even the federal government, have no role in public education. But it does mean that barring good reasons for moving specific decisions in education to higher levels, decision making should remain at the local level, where decisions can be made by those with local experience. Nor should we necessarily assume that the local level means the local district level; in large districts it may well mean that many decisions should be made at an even more local level, at the local community school. The local level, for example, is the best level for deciding who should be hired or retained as teachers, since the local level is where their work is best known and more available for comparison with other teachers. The standards by which teachers are measured, however, should be roughly the same throughout the nation, since the children they educate all have the same general needs.

Shifting decision making to the local level will not be easy. But many of the thorniest problems can be anticipated and resolved. Two of these problems are union suspicions of local decision making and cronyism. Educational decentralization has often brought with it conflicts with unions. Many teachers' unions came into being when local boards were often influenced by racial, religious, and other regional prejudice in hiring and firing, and the legacy of suspicion of local officials lingers. Moreover, unions have often objected to local decision making on hiring, firing, transfers, and promotions because the boards' processes and criteria have often violated the agreements the unions negotiated in master contracts. Catholic social teaching has supported unions since 1891, and feminism has not only supported unions in principle but has worked hard for women's representation in many unions. But support for unions does not necessitate support for centralized educational systems nor opposition to merit-based hiring, firing, or promotion. Rather it means that the criteria on which merit is based must be negotiated between the union and the board. There is no reason why some aspects of teacher contracts, such as salary and benefits, maximum student loads, and length of the work day cannot be negotiated at higher levels, perhaps the state level, and job descriptions, including evaluative criteria, at the local level, as has been done in a few locales.[32] This might well *strengthen* education unions, by giving local union personnel increased opportunity for negotiating their conditions of employment.

Cronyism is another problem that can result from decentralization. Cronyism can extend from favoritism for relatives and friends in hiring to such blatant criminal activity as kickbacks. There is evidence from New York City, for example, that shifting decision making toward community school boards since the late 1960s, away from centralized boards, greatly increased both kinds of cronyism, especially in poor areas. One investigator wrote, "A majority of the city's 32 school boards carved out their districts into fiefdoms where jobs were doled out to loyal campaign workers, lovers, and family or sold for cash."[33] The problem was the worst in poor districts where politicians in general, including those on the school board, were expected to provide jobs for those who work in their campaigns. School personnel and resources were regularly expected to support future campaigns of board members.

But cronyism is preventable. If teacher and principal hiring must meet degree, licensure, and testing requirements; and, even more critical, if principals and teachers are made responsible for student achievement levels; if nepotism rules are established and enforced; and if all schools and school employees are banned from participating in school board elections, then the climate that makes cronyism normative can be broken.[34]

In a number of ways the principle of subsidiarity in education reflects many of the findings of recent research: that the more removed decision making is from people, the less involved those people are with the institution and its activities, and the less effective the institution becomes. Research study after research study has shown that in many different areas of education, children learn better when their parents are involved with their education.[35] Higher achieving schools have higher levels of parent involvement; within individual schools, higher achieving students are more likely to have parents involved with the school. Children whose parents read to them and have their children read to the parents score higher in reading. Sex education programs involving parents and community are more successful in meeting the goals of sex education— increased sexual knowledge, delayed sexual activity, and reduced teen pregnancy—without increasing sexual experimentation.[36] High school dropouts are significantly more likely to have had parents who do not visit, phone, or write teachers to confer about the student.

Involvement of, and decision making by, parents and local community does not, of course, guarantee that good decisions will be made, especially when the parents who become involved represent only one racial, class, or religious group within the society. There are areas of education in which the average parent has more expertise, and others in which most need to collaborate with specialists. For example, parents have long groaned at the stupidity of school boards who staggered class starting times, often to cut costs in transportation, by requiring high schools to begin at 7:00 or 7:30 A.M. and elementary schools as late as 9:00 or 9:30 A.M. Few parents were surprised when recent research demonstrated that teens get their best sleep in the morning hours and learn better later in the day, while younger children wake and learn best earlier. On the other hand, teachers rather than parents were better able to anticipate the conclusions of research that showed that the large middle schools and combined junior/senior high schools with 2,000 or more students (resulting from the school reorganization movement of the 1960s and 1970s) are not nearly so conducive to middle school learning as smaller schools. The larger schools often exacerbate tensions in adolescent identity formation, greatly increase peer pressures, lower concentration levels, and tend to encourage behavior problems.

Subsidiarity does not dictate that education monies must be raised at the most local level, as is presently the case in most of the nation, with schools funded through local property taxes. Nor does subsidiarity dictate that decisions on per capita cost of education be made at the local level. Both solidarity and the general principle of justice would insist that if there are significant differences in the levels of education funding between locales, that those differences be necessary in order to provide more or less equal education. For example, places where it is extremely difficult to attract and retain teachers may need to offer higher salaries to offer students the same education—but where salaries are lower they must still meet just wage requirements. Large, sparsely settled districts will spend more monies on transportation, and some urban districts will spend more on security. But when higher levels of funding in rich districts allow them to have state-of-the-art science facilities, and poorer districts have none and cannot replace outdated science textbooks, solidarity and justice are violated and appeals to subsidiarity are inappropriate.

Many of the calls for educational reform today are calls for experimentation. Catholic social teaching does not dictate that public education must have any one curriculum or organizational framework. Beyond the subsidiarity requirement, social teaching imposes only general goals on education. Education must prepare children for responsible futures of social contribution; it must offer cultural access; and it must not discriminate against any group on the basis of race, sex, class, ethnicity, or religion. Today there is a great deal of ambiguity about what kind of educational system best meets these requirements, and therefore responsible experimentation is appropriate. Not all proposals, however, are responsible in terms of these goals. Even more surely, most of the proposals now on the table may or may not meet these requirements, depending upon the process of implementation. Vouchers and charter schools, for example, can have radically different results, depending upon the specific plan. While there is nothing inherent in the basic framework of either proposal that violates feminist or social teaching principles, so that either or both could be legitimate options, caution is necessary.

The idea behind vouchers is to make the public schools compete for students with private schools, and thereby raise the quality of public schools. And although this could happen, it is most unlikely to occur unless schools that accept vouchers are forbidden to charge additional tuition. Otherwise, parents who could not augment the value of the vouchers with private funds could have very limited choices, often only the local public school. The public schools would then be even more likely to attract only the most economically disadvantaged, which would not encourage competition for excellence—just the opposite. Private schools would not have to discriminate against most "undesirables"; tuition levels would eliminate them. With an unrestricted voucher system, even the relatively inexpensive Catholic and Christian fundamentalist schools would likely raise tuition significantly. With vouchers, private school tuitions could rise up to 100 percent without increasing the cost to present student families. But charging even a few hundred dollars above the voucher would deprive the least affluent 20–25 percent of a viable alternative to the public school. Further, with public funds extended to cover the 12 percent of private school students not presently covered, there would be great political pressure to *lower* the value of vouchers, and thus the amount spent per student in public schools.

Charter schools present a different and more diverse set of possible problems. In many ways charter schools respond to basic values in Catholic social teaching. They represent local initiatives in education, which satisfy the principle of subsidiarity. They would be funded at the level of public schools, which would make them open to all social classes. Important questions about charter schools involve governance and accountability. Charter schools are new, with little in the way of developed models. Many states' charter laws do not specify how charter schools fit into the public school system. Their autonomy from local districts and boards in personnel matters, capital expenses, supply ordering, as well as their receipt of operational and categorical funds from state and federal governments is in question in most states.[37]

Accountability procedures are just as weak. There is an absence of agreed-upon measures of achievement promised in the charters. Many charter schools merely present folios of student work as evidence of meeting the charter goals; there are no methods for comparing this work with students' previous work or with the work of students in non-charter schools.[38]

Christine E. Gudorf

Questions about charter schools also include how to draw lines about what objectives in schools should be publicly funded. Should there be publicly funded schools developed by Catholics, Jews, Seventh-Day Adventists, Baptists, Muslims, Christian Scientists, Lakota Sioux, and Haitian Voudouists? How about Christian Identity, the National Organization of Women, the Nation of Islam, Islamic Jihad, the NAACP, the Klan, or the Communist Party? All of these groups will have different perspectives from which history and governance should be taught, literature selected, and citizenship and moral behavior advocated. Presumably all would teach basic literacy and math skills. Some conservative advocates of charter schools argue that so long as the schools reach the specific education goals of the charter, there should be no interference in or objections to them. This would seem to give public support to education tinged with hate and violence, and be inimical to the common good. Many liberals, on the other hand, argue that public education should be secular education, though this seems to transform American separation of church and state from the mutual protection outlined in the First Amendment into a preference for secularist society, and some would insist a preference for atheist society.

Catholic social teaching lifts up the common good as the appropriate goal for individuals and society, insists on the dignity and equality of all persons, as well as sets rigid limits on the use of violence.[39] Feminism, too, would deny public funds to any group that teaches the inequality or subordination of any group. If the goal of educational policy is the common good, then no public school can be allowed to teach hate or disrespect for any group, though no group should be made to ignore or minimize historical injustices toward them in order to avoid being labeled hate mongerers. All public schools should teach respect for peace and a commitment to work for justice through civil procedures, reserving recourse to violence for those very rare instances of communal last resort where the risks of violence do not outweigh the seriousness of the injustice to be righted. But compliance with these criteria would need to be enforced in an ongoing way if charter schools are to live up to the public trust.

The other oft-raised question about charter schools—which could also be relevant to vouchers—is more difficult. What would be the social effect of supporting narrow religious, political, and social points of view in both home and school, so that young adults are deprived of mixing with youngsters of other groups? It could be a problem. But I suspect that for the most part the United States is already too undifferentiated and integrated for this to be a widespread problem in areas other than race. The number of charter schools that are exclusively Amish, Rumanian, Haitian Voudouist, Hassidic Jewish, or even Christian Identity will be very small, and most of those that might come to be will share the majority of society's concerns about basic skills, computer literacy, and sex education, and will fairly rapidly develop their own internal divisions over these and other issues in education and childrearing. Secularization is too far advanced among American religious communities to support large-scale separatism; few of us define ourselves solely in terms of narrow religious-ethnic group identities. We want our children's education to prepare them for careers and for citizenship as well as for religious and family life, for responsible decision making and self-fulfillment in a rapidly changing pluralist world. Very few Americans are convinced, or are likely to be convinced, that public education limited by narrow, separatist religio-ethnic traditions oriented to the past are in our children's best interest—unless they and their children are so rejected by the larger society that such separation seems required as a survival tactic. On the other hand, I cannot stress too much the possibility of charter schools and voucher programs for increasing racial segregation in the United States. Implementation plans for any of these experiments should keep a critical eye on the effects of the program on racial segregation within both the experiment itself and the local public schools, and revise policies as necessary.

Neither feminism nor Catholic social teaching offers a blueprint for exactly what should be done in education. Rather they offer us general guidance about the quality of social life for which we should aim and the appropriate role of education within that social life. The Catholic community in the United States needs to begin an internal dialogue about the shape of public education and the appropriate relationship between public and parochial schools in light of its commitment to the common good of the American people. The initial topics in that dialogue should be, If

Catholic schools become charter schools, or all students receive vouchers, what portion of the Catholic public schools students will shift to the Catholic schools in any given locale, and how will that affect racial segregation?

Using Toynbee's famous distinction between the self-image and behavior of churches and sects,[40] the shift in the status and numbers of Catholics in the United States demands that the Catholic Church stop thinking of itself as a beleaguered and powerless immigrant *sect* whose first concern must be the welfare of its own members and instead consider itself as the single largest U.S. *church,* with responsibilities to the entire nation as well as to its own members. The U.S. church has already made this shift in many other areas of social teaching, including nuclear warfare, the economy, capital punishment, health care, and racial justice—now is the time to do it in regard to public education.

Notes

1. I recognize that there is at least one other difference that separates Catholic and feminist politics (though not theory): that concerning the pursuit of power. Feminism assumes that people legitimately pursue power, which is not inherently domination, but is rather the exercise of personal potential and responsibility (Nancy Hartsock, *The Feminist Standpoint and Other Essays,* Boulder, CO: Westview, 1988, 15–20). Church politics has up to and including the present exhibited unease at power directly exercised by the masses. Demands for, and pursuit of, power by women have similarly been viewed as demeaning the dignity of women, as unbecoming to femininity. There is, in short, a preference in church politics for the powerful to protect

the interests of the weak, to understand the preferential option for the poor as aimed at the non-poor. (See William I. Robinson, *Promoting Polyarchy: Globalization, U.S. Intervention and Hegemony,* Cambridge/New York/Melbourne: Cambridge University Press, 1996, 117–316, for descriptions of Catholic politics on the masses.)

2. *Acta Apostolicae Sedis* 22 (1930): 549–50; translation: *Papal Teaching: Matrimony* (Boston: Daughters of St. Paul, 1963), 258–59.

3. Paul VI, *Ricordi Antichi* (Address to the Union of Italian Catholic Jurists), December 8, 1974; *Osservatore Romano,* December 8, 1974; translation: *The Pope Speaks,* Vol. 19, 314–16.

4. John Paul II, *Mulieris Dignitatem (On the Dignity and Vocation of Women),* August 15, 1988 (Washington, DC: U.S. Catholic Conference, 1988), no. 24.

5. Joseph W. Newman, "Comparing Private Schools and Public Schools in the Twentieth Century: History, Demography, and the Debate over Choice," *Educational Foundations* (Summer 1995): 11–13.

6. Ibid., 14.

7. Ibid., 8, citing studies by Buetow (1970), Coleman and Hoffer (1987), and Byrk et al. (1993).

8. Ibid., 8.

9. Ibid., 11.

10. "Failed Students Get to Keep Diplomas," *Miami Herald,* February 28, 1998, 2B; Jacqueline Charles and Sabrina Walters, "Students' Low GPAs May Spell Failure; Thousands Won't Receive Diplomas," *Miami Herald,* April 3, 1998, 1A.

11. Jodi Mailander Farrell, "How School Rated Worst Beat the System," *Miami Herald,* June 28, 1998, 1A.

12. "Massachusetts Tests Aspiring Teachers Colleges," *Providence Journal,* July 24, 1998, A16.

13. Pam Belluck, "Free-Spending in Flush Times Is Coming Back to Haunt States," *New York Times* online, March 9, 2001.

14. "Lessons: Getting Good Teachers for Poor Schools," *New York Times* online, September 20, 2000.
15. Abby Goodnough, "Metro Briefing: New York: Brooklyn: Educators Get Pay Bonus," *New York Times* online, June 28, 2001.
16. Barbara Whitaker, "School Improvements Are Cited in California," *New York Times* online, October 5, 2000.
17. "Texas District Solves Teacher Shortage," *Curriculum Review* 29 (February 1990): 1, p. 18.
18. There are at least two varieties of vouchers proposed: restricted and unrestricted, though the areas that have introduced vouchers—Minnesota and Cleveland—both have restricted access. Milton Friedman proposes that all parents be issued vouchers ("Public Schools: Make Them Private," *Education Economics* 5, no. 3 (1997): 341–44), while Jack Coons and Steven Sugarman of the University of California-Berkeley Law School argue that vouchers should go only to those students most disadvantaged by the current public education system, particularly those in the inner cities ("The Private School Option in Systems of Education Choice," *Educational Leadership* 48, no. 4 (Dec 1990/Jan 1991): 54–56.
19. See, for example, the role of justice in Diana L. Hayes, "My Hope Is in the Lord: Transformation and Salvation in the African-American Community," in Emilie Townes, ed., *Embracing the Spirit: Womanist Perspectives on Hope, Salvation and Transformation* (Maryknoll, NY: Orbis, 1997), 9–28; Katie G. Canon, *Katie's Canon: Womanism and the Soul of the Black Community* (New York Continuum, 1995), 54–55; Barbara Andolson, "A Woman's Work Is Never Done: Unpaid Household Labor as a Social Justice Issue"; Joan Griscom, "On Healing the Nature/History Split in Feminist Thought"; and Starhawk, "Ethics and Justice in Goddess Religion," in Andolson et al., *Women's Consciousness, Women's Conscience: A Reader in*

Christine E. Gudorf

Feminist Ethics (Minneapolis, MN: Winston-Seabury, 1985), and many others which place justice at the center of feminist demands. The dichotomy that developed between justice as a (male) principle opposed to a female ethic of care following publication of Carol Gilligan's *In A Different Voice* (Cambridge, MA: Harvard University Press, 1984) was misleading, in that feminists have never been convinced that justice and care are mutually exclusive, only that women were socialized to integrate more generalized care into action for justice than were men who were socialized toward more abstract principled interpretations and pursuit of justice.

20. Hartsock, *Feminist Standpoint*, 36.
21. Second Vatican Council, *Gaudium et Spes, 69*.
22. Paul VI, *Populorum Progressio,* 22.
23. John Paul II, *Sollicitudo Rei Socialis,* 38.
24. Ibid.
25. "Address to the Indians of Oaxaca and Chiapas," in Alfred T. Hennelly, ed., *Liberation Theology: A Documentary History* (Maryknoll, NY: Orbis, 1990), 260–61.
26. See, for example, the many works of Rosemary Radford Ruether and Elisabeth Schüssler Fiorenza, to name but two of the best-known feminist writers in this area.
27. Leo insisted that because work was not only personal but also necessary to support life, the worker's acceptance of less than a just wage is a matter of force and injustice (Leo XIII, *Rerum Novarum,* 34).
28. See, for example, Rosita deAnn Mathews, "Using Power from the Periphery: An Alternative Theological Model for Survival in Systems," and M. Shawn Copeland, "Wading Through Many Sorrows: Toward a Theology of Suffering in Womanist Perspective," both in Emilie Townes, ed., *A Troubling in My Soul: Womanist Perspectives on Evil and Suffering* (Maryknoll, NY: Orbis, 1993). Katie Canon surveyed the situation of black women from the seventeenth through the

twentieth centuries in the United States and concluded, "The moral situation of the Black woman in contemporary society is still a situation of struggle, a struggle to survive collectively and individually against the continuing harsh historical realities and pervasive adversities in today's world" (*Black Womanist Ethics,* Atlanta, GA: Scholar's Press, 1988, 66).

29. Congregation for the Doctrine of the Faith, "Instructions on Christian Faith and Liberation," *Origins* 15 (April 17, 1986): 44.

30. Paul VI, *Populorum Progressio,* 35.

31. John Paul II, *Centesimus Annus,* 33.

32. C. Kerchner, J. Koppich, and J. Weaver, *United Mind Workers: Unions and Teaching in the Knowledge Society* (San Francisco: Jossey-Bass, 1997).

33. Lydia Segal, "The Pitfalls of Political Decentralization and Proposals for Reform: The Case of New York City Public Schools," *Public Administration Review* 57 (March/April 1997): 2, 141.

34. Lydia Segal, "Pitfalls of Political Decentralization," 147–49; Julia Koppich, "Considering Non-Traditional Alternatives: Charters, Private Contracts and Vouchers," *Financing Schools* 17 (Winter 1997): 3, 100, 105; "Principal Principles," *New Republic,* January 5–12, 1998, 7; Anthony Bryk, Paul E. Deabster, John Q. Easton, Stuart Luppescu, and Yeow Meng Thum, "Measuring Achievement Gains in the Chicago Public Schools," *Education and Urban Society* 26 (May 1994): 3, 306–19; Thomas A. Downes and Jaculyn Horowitz, "Analysis of the Effect of Chicago School Reform on Student Performance," *Economic Perspectives* (1995): 2, 13–33.

35. Rebecca A. Marcon, "Doing the Right Thing by Children: Linking Research and Public Policy Reform in the District of Columbia Public Schools," *Young Children,* November 1994, 17–18.

36. D. Kirby, *Sexuality Education: An Evaluation of Programs and Their Effects—Executive Summary* (Bethesda, MD:

Mathtech, Inc., 1984); M. Vincent et al., "Reducing Adolescent Pregnancy Through School and Community-Based Education," *Journal of the American Medical Association* 257 (1987): 24, 3382–86; D. Cors-Bramble et al., "The Sex Education Practicum: Medical Students in the Elementary School Classroom," *Journal of School Health* 62 (1992): 32–34.

37. Koppich, 102.
38. Ibid., 100.
39. Specifically, Catholic just war thought lists seven conditions to be met before engagement in organized violence can be just, and two restrictions on violent activity within a just war.
40. Arnold Toynbee, *Christianity Among the Religions of the World* (Scribner's, 1957).

List of Contributors

LISA SOWLE CAHILL is the J. Donald Monan Professor of Theology at Boston College, where she has taught since 1976. She received her doctorate at the University of Chicago Divinity School. Among her publications are *Sex, Gender, and Christian Ethics; Women and Sexuality;* and *Between the Sexes.* She is past president of the Catholic Theological Society of America. She has five children, three of whom were adopted from Thailand.

M. SHAWN COPELAND is associate professor of theology at Marquette University and (adjunct) associate professor of systematic theology at the Institute for Black Catholic Studies, Xavier University of Louisiana. She received her doctoral degree from Boston College and is author of more than sixty articles, reviews, and commentaries in professional journals and books on topics such as suffering, identity and difference, the common human good and freedom.

MARGARET A. FARLEY, R.S.M., holds the Gilbert L. Stark Chair in Christian Ethics at the Divinity School of Yale University, where she received her doctorate. She is author or co-editor of five books and multiple articles on topics in theological ethics, medical ethics, sexual ethics, and feminist ethics. She is past president of the Society of Christian Ethics as well as the Catholic Theological Society of America.

CHRISTINE E. GUDORF is professor of Religious Studies at Florida International University in Miami. She earned her Ph.D. in Religion from Columbia University and taught at Xavier University for fifteen years before accepting a position at Florida International in 1993. She has published six books and many articles in areas of Christian ethics, feminist ethics, and liberation theologies.

ROSEMARY LULING HAUGHTON was cofounder in 1981 of Wellspring House, Inc., in Gloucester, Massachusetts. It has gained acclaim for its pioneer work for social justice, providing family sheltering, education, housing, and economic opportunities, and for public policy work. Among her best-known books are *The Transformation of Man; The Catholic Thing; Song in a Strange Land;* and *Images for Change.* She is the mother of ten children and several foster children.

MARY AQUIN O'NEILL, R.S.M., is founding director of the Mount Saint Agnes Theological Center for Women in Baltimore, Maryland (www.msawomen.org). She received her doctoral degree from Vanderbilt University. She has taught at Mount Saint Agnes College, Vanderbilt University, Loyola College of Maryland, Salve Regina College, and the University of Notre Dame. Mary Aquin has lectured in

Jerusalem, Australia, Argentina, and throughout the United States and has published in a variety of theological journals.

MAGDALA THOMPSON, R.S.M., is an individual, marriage, and family therapist in private practice in Mobile, Alabama. She received her Ph.D. at Michigan State University. Prior to opening a practice she served in administration at Auburn University, Alabama; Mount Saint Agnes and Loyola Colleges, Maryland; and Michigan State University. With Thomas E. Clarke, S.J., and W. Harold Grant, she published *From Image to Likeness: A Jungian Path in the Gospel Journey.*